Aidan

of Lindisfarne

Published by The Langley Press, 2022

To Judith and Rob Catty

Aidan

of Lindisfarne

by

Simon Webb

Also from the Langley Press

In Search of Bede

Bede's Life of Saint Cuthbert

The Legend of Saint Cuthbert

The Voyage of Saint Brendan

The Legend of the Three Kings

In Search of Saint Alban

The Passion of Saint Edmund

A Little Book of English Saints

Gilbert's Tale: The Life and Death of Thomas Becket

For more books from the Langley Press,
please visit our website at:

www.langleypress.co.uk.

CONTENTS

Bede, from a twelfth century manuscript in the British Library

Introduction

The trunk and some of the branches of this book are borrowed from the Venerable Bede. Bede was a monk and scholar who lived in Northumbria in the late seventh and early eighth centuries, dying at Jarrow in 735, at the age of sixty-one or sixty-two. He is now regarded as a saint, and one of the celebrated Doctors of the Church, a title he shares with the likes of Pope Gregory the Great, St Augustine of Hippo and St Jerome. Pilgrims can visit Bede's tomb in the Galilee chapel of Durham Cathedral, but in his *Divine Comedy* the Italian poet Dante Alighieri put Bede's immortal soul in the fourth sphere of heaven, in the sun itself, together with King Solomon, Boethius, Thomas Aquinas and others.

Bede wrote on a bewildering variety of subjects, including education, the lives of the saints, the meaning of the Bible and the calculation of the correct date of Easter. He also wrote poetry, but by far his best-known work is the *Ecclesiastical History of the English People*, first written in Latin and completed around the year 731.

According to Henry Mayr-Harting, author of the 2004 UK Dictionary of National Biography article on St Aidan, 'all that is known about [Aidan] comes from Bede's *Historia ecclesiastica*'. The many gaps in Bede's account of Aidan explain why parts of my biography of Aidan comprise speculations about what may have happened in the gaps, and explorations of what we cannot know for sure about the saint. Although Bede wrote a whole book about Aidan's younger contemporary St Cuthbert, he opted to set Aidan in the context of his *Historia*, which meant that he really didn't have much space to dedicate to this extraordinary, pivotal man.

In English translation, the *Historia* occupies fewer that three hundred pages. Into this space the chronicler chose to fit nearly eight hundred years of English history. In order to set his story in context, Bede was also obliged to cover events that happened outside of England, particularly in Rome, France, Wales, Ireland and what we now call Scotland. Bede's task was further complicated by the fact that, as we shall see, England was not a unified country in his day. He had to touch on the histories of many small, separate English kingdoms.

The result is that Bede is able to tell us comparatively little about Aidan. Since the chronicler must have been working from some sources that are now lost, we have no way of knowing for sure whether he *could* have written more about Aidan, for instance if he had opted to write a stand-alone biography of the saint, or if he had decided to greatly increase the overall length of his *Historia*.

Whatever sources Bede used to construct his historical sketch of Aidan, the chronicler seems not to have been familiar with some old Irish texts that provide possible details of the saint's life before he arrived in Northumbria in 635. It is possible that, before he became Abbot and Bishop of Lindisfarne, Aidan filled the same position on another monastic island, Scattery Island in the Shannon Estuary. He is also supposed to have been a disciple of St Senan, the founder of the monastery there, but some sources suggest that Senan died nearly fifty years before Aidan was born. Certainly Senan seems to belong more to the mythological side of Irish church history than his supposed disciple Aidan. He is said to have rid Scattery of a dangerous monster before he set up his monastery there, and sought to guarantee the celibacy of his monks by forbidding any woman to stay there. This presented a problem when his own sister begged to be buried on the island: Senan got round the problem by burying her on a part of Scattery that was under water at high tide. Senan's sister was therefore buried on the island, and not buried on the island, making her a little like Schrödinger's celebrated cat; both dead and not dead.

As well as lamenting the comparative scarcity of material about his subject in the *Historia*, the biographer of Aidan also has to bear in mind the distinctive character and point of view of Bede's chronicle. If the roots of my book on Aidan are the truth, 'what actually happened', the metaphor works because the roots of a tree usually remain underground. Bede cannot be relied on to give us the truth as defined by modern historians. Although in the preface to his *Historia*, addressed to its dedicatee King Ceolwulf of Northumbria, Bede claims to 'have laboured to commit to writing such things as I could gather from common report, for the instruction of posterity' (trans. A.M. Sellar, 1907), there are certain marked biases in his approach, and earlier in the same preface Bede mentions motivations for his writing that would seem alien to many modern historians:

If history relates good things of good men, the attentive hearer is excited to imitate that which is good; or if it recounts evil things of wicked persons, none the less the conscientious and devout hearer

9

or reader, shunning that which is hurtful and wrong, is the more earnestly fired to perform those things which he knows to be good, and worthy of the service of God.

Bede's assertion that history could be written with the intention of leading people towards virtue and away from evil may sound a little vague, but it is likely that the chronicler had some specific examples in mind. Throughout his history, Bede is keen to point up how pious kings like Ceolwulf can help promote Christianity and thus, from Bede's point of view, improve the lives (and after-lives) of their subjects. In a letter to Bishop Egbert of York, written in 734, Bede implied that his correspondent could be a better bishop, if only he would take advantage of the help offered by the pious King Ceolwulf.

In his history, Bede also reminds us how the Roman Emperor Constantine the Great promoted the Christian cause, and how Lucius, a second-century king of the Britons wrote to Pope Eleutherius (died 189 CE) asking for help to make his kingdom a Christian one. King Lucius who, as we will see, may never have existed, became a surprisingly hot topic at the time of the English Reformation. The Protestants claimed that this, the first known Christian king of the Britons, made himself the ruler of his local Church, as King Henry VIII intended to do. By contrast, the Roman Catholics claimed that the fact that Lucius had written to the Pope showed that he understood that the papacy was supreme, and that no local monarch should run the Church. Lucius's name was dragged into the trial of the Catholic martyr John Boste at Durham in 1594. Francis Beaumont, the biased judge at the trial, claimed that the pope who regularly corresponded with Lucius had told the British king that the Church would not assume much power over the affairs of his kingdom.

Bede's *Historia* is peppered with other pious kings, including Sigeberht of the East Angles, a seventh-century monarch who abdicated in order to become a monk, as Ceolwulf also opted to do. The potentially very productive relationship between a sympathetic king and a motivated Christian missionary is central to the story of Aidan, who worked under three kings: Oswald, Oswiu and Oswine.

In the *Historia*, Bede's idea of history as a source of useful examples to guide the life-choices of his readers is coupled with a clear intention to show that characters and events from English history might be sufficiently interesting and important to allow comparison with their equivalents in the annals of the Roman Empire, and in the Bible. In a passage on King Ethelfrith of Northumbria, a predecessor of Ceolwulf's and the father of Aidan's patron King Oswald, Bede compared Ethelfrith:

to Saul of old, king of the Israelites, save only in this, that he [Ethelfrith] was ignorant of Divine religion. For he conquered more territories from the Britons than any other chieftain or king, either subduing the inhabitants and making them tributary, or driving them out and planting the English in their places. To him might justly be applied the saying of the patriarch blessing his son in the person of Saul, "Benjamin shall ravin as a wolf; in the morning he shall devour the prey, and at night he shall divide the spoil".

Bede's tendency to turn to the Bible in this way is entirely consistent with his status as a monk, as is his determination to keep his history an ecclesiastical history, however much his modern readers might want him to write less about the miracles of local saints and more about the lives of Anglo-Saxon monarchs, warriors, craftsmen and peasants. Other tendencies as revealed in the *Historia* show that Bede was a monk committed to what we would now call the Roman Catholic way. This meant that when he addressed figures such as Aidan, whose background was in the rival, Celtic tradition of Christianity, a marked note of disapproval could creep into his writing.

If the trunk and many of the branches of this book are borrowed from Bede, the other branches come from other sources, not so much on Aidan, but on his times, the people and places he knew, and the personalities, texts and traditions that influenced him. Critics, who might be tempted to amuse themselves by cutting down my book with their metaphorical axes, may want to dismiss all this as 'background'. To them I would say that we all live our lives against a background, and that Aidan's background is both unfamiliar to many modern readers, and also unusually interesting. Like many of the more influential characters from history, Aidan deliberately changed his background or setting, abandoning his comfort-zone and attempting to embed himself and his message in a culture that was quite new to him.

Other historic personages who had to change background before they were able to make a significant contribution to the world would include St Columba, the founder of Aidan's monastery on the island of Iona; St Patrick, the apostle of the Irish, and St Cuthbert, whose bones lie at the other end of Durham Cathedral from Bede's. After a lukewarm reception back home in Nazareth, Jesus observed that a prophet has no honour in his own country (John 4:44): he had had to leave Galilee to make an impact. In the Old Testament, we also have the example of Moses, who could only really emerge as a leader of the Israelites after he had left Egypt with them. Abram's experience was similar: he had to leave Ur to become Abraham, the great patriarch (Genesis 12:1).

The idea that the truth might be compared to a tree's underground root-system is a reminder that many of our newer sources on Aidan's time have emerged from archaeological digs. One site in particular, Sutton Hoo in Sussex, has told us a lot about English life in Aidan's era, since it was first discovered on the eve of the Second World War. More recent discoveries in Staffordshire and Norfolk have shed additional light on this period, and historians have worked to connect these new finds to what was already extant from the Anglo-Saxon period, in the form of both texts and artefacts.

St Oswald by Matthew Paris (BL)

I: Oswald Prepares the Ground

Any account of the life of Aidan must begin with his royal patron, Oswald. Oswald is one of the saintly kings of the English. The list also includes Edwin, Ethelbert, Edmund, Alfred the Great, Edward the Confessor, Sigeberht (whom we have already met) and Ceolwulf, the king to whom Bede dedicated his *Ecclesiastical History*. All of these were Anglo-Saxon kings, though England also has both male and female royal saints who lived after the Norman Conquest. Among the saintly kings of the Anglo-Saxons, only Edward the Confessor was considered to be king of England. The rest ruled parts of what would later become a more united country. Like Ceolwulf, and his uncle Edwin, Oswald ruled Northumbria, while Ethelbert ruled Kent, Edmund and Sigeberht East Anglia, and Alfred, Wessex.

These areas, including Northumbria, the windswept region to the north of the River Humber, were parts of what historians used to call the Anglo-Saxon heptarchy, or seven kingdoms. The kingdoms that made up the rest of the seven were Mercia, Essex and Sussex. The seven kingdoms were bordered to the west by Wales and Cornwall (though Cornwall was part of England by the time of Edward the Confessor) and to the north by Scotland.

The power of the Anglo-Saxon kings was often challenged from outside the seven kingdoms by the Scots and Picts, and by the Britons in Wales. The Scots, Picts and Britons, in contrast to the Anglo-Saxons, were long considered to be Celtic peoples, though now historians believe that many of them may have been descended from indigenous peoples who pre-dated the arrival of the Celtic culture on our shores. The idea of the Anglo-Saxon heptarchy has also been challenged by recent research, which suggests that the picture was more complex than old maps of the heptarchy might suggest.

It is as well to remember that the Scots, after whom Scotland is now named, were originally from Ireland. In Aidan's day, 'Scotia' meant Ireland itself, but from the fifth century the Irish Scots or 'Scoti' spread from the north of Ireland into the west of what we now call Scotland. Their kingdom, which lay on both sides of the North Channel, was known as Dalriada. Crucially for the story of Aidan, it included the islands of the Inner Hebrides, including Iona. It was not until the reign of the ninth century Scottish king Kenneth I MacAlpin that the lands of the Scots to the west and the Picts to the east were united to form the kingdom of Alba.

It cannot be said that the seven Anglo-Saxon kingdoms that formed the heptarchy shared England peacefully, or that their royal saints always behaved in a saintly way. Theirs was a warlike culture, obsessed with battle: even members of the same royal family fought against each other. Edwin became king of Northumbria by waging war against his brother-in-law King Ethelfrith (compared to the Old Testament King Saul by Bede) who died during a battle by the River Idle in Nottinghamshire, perhaps in the year 616 CE.

During Edwin's reign, King Ethelfrith's sons, and many of the younger nobility of Northumbria, lived in exile among the Scots or Picts, where they learned about what we now call Celtic Christianity, and were baptised. The names of Ethelfrith's sons were Eanfrith, Oswald, Oswiu, Oswudu, Oslac, Oslaf and Offa (not the king of Mercia of the same name, who built Offa's Dyke). Meanwhile King Edwin himself embraced Christianity, like his enemies, the sons of Ethelfrith. He had learned about the new faith in the court of his ally, Readwald, the king of the East Angles. Without Readwald's help, it is unlikely that Edwin would have been able to assume the Northumbrian throne at all.

Despite the Christian atmosphere of Readwald's court, it seems that Edwin did not formally convert to Christianity, and get baptised, until he had his feet under the table as king of Northumbria. It may be that he hesitated to turn up as the new king of a largely pagan kingdom, with a new faith that might alienate his new subjects. In any case, his subjects might already resent him for having deposed Ethelfrith. As king, Edwin consulted with his courtiers about the idea of converting his whole kingdom: it seems there was never really a question of Edwin personally getting baptised, while his new subjects remained pagan, or were allowed to choose for themselves. They were expected to follow their monarch to the font.

By the time of his baptism Edwin had married his second wife, Ethelburh, a Christian princess from Kent. She had brought with her her chaplain, Bishop Paulinus, who was probably part of the second wave of missionaries sent from Rome to convert the English. Perhaps under the influence of Paulinus, at least two of Edwin's followers showed that they were in favour of the switch to Christianity. Bede tells us that a pagan priest called Coifi took the opportunity to complain about the pagan gods, who had done him no favours, and also to hint that Edwin himself might have treated him (Coifi) better in the past:

O king, consider what this is which is now preached to us; for I verily declare to you what I have learnt beyond doubt, that the religion which we have hitherto professed has no virtue in it and no profit. For none of your people has applied himself more diligently to the worship of our gods than I; and yet there are many who receive greater favours from you, and are more preferred than I, and are more prosperous in all that they undertake to do or to get. Now if the gods were good for any thing, they would rather forward me, who have been careful to serve them with greater zeal. It remains, therefore, that if upon examination you find those new doctrines, which are now preached to us, better and more efficacious, we hasten to receive them without any delay.

While Coifi was evidently looking for a new god who might help him out in practical ways, an unnamed courtier of Edwin's, a man who surely possessed the heart of a true poet, sought a cure for what we might call existential angst. 'The present life of man upon earth, O king,' he began,

seems to me, in comparison with that time which is unknown to us, like to the swift flight of a sparrow through the house wherein you sit at supper in winter, with your ealdormen and thegns, while the fire blazes in the midst, and the hall is warmed, but the wintry storms of rain or snow are raging abroad. The sparrow, flying in at one door and immediately out at another, whilst he is within, is safe from the wintry tempest; but after a short space of fair weather, he immediately vanishes out of your sight, passing from winter into winter again. So this life of man appears for a little while, but of what is to follow or what went before we know nothing at all. If, therefore, this new doctrine tells us something more certain, it seems justly to deserve to be followed.

The powerful image of life as the short time spent by a tiny bird, flying through an Anglo-Saxon mead-hall, is perhaps the most striking idea in the whole of Bede's *Ecclesiastical History*. If nothing else, the passage gives us an evocative bird's-eye view of such a place, at the height of a king's power. When Edwin at last embraced Christianity, Coifi rode about like a madman, desecrating the old pagan temples and destroying the idols.

Edwin's rule was challenged by an alliance of the Mercians under their king, Penda, and their British allies under Cadwallon ap Cadfan, king of Gwynedd in North Wales. In 633, Edwin died at the Battle of Hatfield Chase near Doncaster: his sparrow-life had flown out into the night. On Edwin's death, Northumbria split into two separate kingdoms (as it had a tendency to do), Bernicia to the north and Deira in the south. The city of Durham lies somewhere in the area where the two kingdoms were divided, though the boundaries between the Anglo-Saxon kingdoms were never strictly defined.

After Edwin's death, Ethelfrith's sons were allowed to return home, and Eanfrith, the eldest brother, became king of Bernicia, while Osric ruled Deira. As soon as they had mounted their earthly thrones, both of these brothers abandoned their Christianity and resumed the paganism of their ancestors. This must have been easier, and more tempting, in seventh-century Northumbria than it would have been anywhere in England later in the Middle Ages. At the time, the pagan religion of the Anglo-Saxons predominated in many areas, and Penda, the

Mercian king who had unseated Edwin, was himself a pagan. The temporary disappearance of Christianity in the areas ruled by Oswald's brothers suggests that the new religion had only ever been skin-deep there. Edwin and Paulinus had, so to speak, painted the front door a new colour. When Aidan arrived, he set about re-building the whole house.

Little is known about the pre-Christian beliefs of the Anglo-Saxons, but the pagan heritage of the English still survives in some of our names for days of the week. Tuesday, for instance, was named for the war-god Tiu, Wednesday for Woden and Thursday for Thor. Some English place-names are also derived from the names of pagan deities, such as Wednesbury in the West Midlands, where there must once have been a shrine to Woden. The words 'Yule' and 'Easter' also have pagan origins. The kings of Northumbria, like Edwin and Oswald, claimed descent from Woden. Since Queen Elizabeth II is supposed to be descended from the kings of Wessex, who also claimed descent from this pagan god, her majesty must also have both divine and royal blood.

Oswald's link to Woden did not consist only in his supposed descent from this Germanic version of the Roman Jupiter. The Northumbrian king was also associated with a raven, and is often depicted with one of these birds on his wrist. A modern banner currently hanging by the grave of St Cuthbert in Durham cathedral shows Oswald riding a white horse, with a sword in one hand and a raven on the other. This is a reference to the story, found in Bede's *Ecclesiastical History*, of the raven that rescued Oswald's severed arm from the battlefield, perhaps at Oswestry in Shropshire, where he died in 642. The bird hung the arm in an ash tree, where it proved to be impervious to decay, remaining 'incorrupt'.

A raven also features earlier in Oswald's story: the reason why the ravens that accompany the saint-king in pictures are often holding rings in their beaks is because a talking raven acted as a go-between for Oswald and his future wife when they were courting. In this role, the bird conveyed the gift of a ring to Oswald from Princess Kyneburga, daughter of the king of Wessex. Oswald's supposed ancestor Woden had two ravens, called Huginn and Munnin, or Thought and Memory, which sat on his shoulders. They were able to speak human language, and flew all over the world like modern reconnaissance drones collecting information for their master. Oswald's resemblance to his ancestor Woden may explain some of the saint's medieval popularity in German-speaking countries.

Although modern readers might be intrigued and even charmed by stories about the pre-Christian gods of the English, Bede associated paganism with idol-worship, defilement and abomination. The chronicler disapproved of the course Osric and Eanfrith took in reverting to paganism: he also had little time for the mixed approach of Readwald, the ally of the brothers' uncle Edwin. Although he had been baptised into the Christian faith, Bede tells us that Readwald's wife persuaded him to worship the pagan gods as well. He set up altars for pagan animal sacrifices right next to Christian altars, thus hedging his spiritual bets. Readwald may have been the king buried in the Sutton Hoo ship burial, which includes both Christian and pagan elements.

Readwald's compromise with paganism is reminiscent of the backsliding of King Solomon, as recounted in the Old Testament:

For it came to pass, when Solomon was old, that his wives turned away his heart after other gods: and his heart was not perfect with the Lord his God, as was the heart of David his father. For Solomon went after Ashtoreth the goddess of the Zidonians, and after Milcom the abomination of the Ammonites. And Solomon did evil in the sight of the Lord, and went not fully after the Lord, as did David his father. Then did Solomon build an high place for Chemosh, the abomination of Moab, in the hill that is before Jerusalem, and for Molech, the abomination of the children of Ammon. And likewise did he for all his strange wives, which burnt incense and sacrificed unto their gods.

(1 Kings 11, 4-8, KJV)

Though they had turned their backs on Jesus, Osric and Eanfrith soon had to face Cadwallon of Gwynedd, who had been part of the alliance that had unseated their uncle Edwin. The Welsh king was holed up in York when Osric rashly laid siege to the city. Cadwallon sallied out with all the forces at his disposal, killed Osric and destroyed his entire army.

The king of Gwynedd followed up his victory at York by occupying Northumbria for a whole year, ruling not like a benevolent king, but in the style of a greedy tyrant. He fooled Eanfrith into coming to him with a bodyguard of only twelve soldiers, ostensibly to negotiate a peace. Eanfrith never left the meeting alive.

That terrible year, when the royal brothers turned from their faith, and the king of Gwynedd ravaged their kingdoms, was remembered as an ill-omened and hateful time. It was agreed that Osric and Eanfrith should be omitted from the official list of English kings, and the dark year allotted to the next king, their brother Oswald.

After the death of Eanfrith, Oswald set out with an army that Bede tells us was certainly small, but reinforced with the power of Christian faith. Cadwallon had a much larger force, which he claimed could never be defeated. Nevertheless the British chief was slain in battle against Oswald. The place was still venerated in Bede's time, not just because it was the site of Oswald's victory, but also because he had erected a makeshift cross there, just before the battle commenced. Oswald himself held the cross straight while his followers piled earth around the base to steady it. This may have been the first time that a Christian symbol had ever been used as a battle-standard in that part of Britain. Oswald knelt down by the cross and prayed to heaven for help in the clash that was about to commence.

He cried out to his soldiers, 'Let us all kneel, and beg the true and living God Almighty in his mercy to defend us from the proud and cruel enemy: he knows we are waging a just war, to save our nation!' After they had prayed, the host advanced on the enemy at dawn.

The story of the cross Oswald erected at Heavenfield near Hexham is reminiscent of one of the more famous stories that have attached themselves to Constantine, the first Roman emperor to encourage the spread of Christianity throughout his empire. Before the battle of the Milvian Bridge in Rome in 312 CE, Constantine was told in a vision to have a Christian symbol painted on his soldiers' shields. Whether this sign was a kind of cross, or the Ch-Rho symbol, made up of the first two letters of the word 'Christ' in Greek is unclear. In any case Constantine won the battle, which allowed him to go on to become emperor. His time in office did no end of good for the Christian cause.

And Constantine had a special link to Britain: he had been declared emperor at York in 306 CE, and some claimed that his mother Helena was British. Heavenfield, where Oswald erected his cross, is close to a section of Hadrian's Wall, begun nearly two hundred years before Constantine was proclaimed emperor at York.

Like Constantine, Oswald had an encouraging vision before the crucial battle that he fought using a Christian symbol. Adamnan, a seventh-century abbot of the monastery on Iona, tells us that while:

. . . this same King Oswald, after pitching his camp, in readiness for the battle, was sleeping one day on a pillow in his tent, he saw St Columba in a vision, beaming with angelic brightness, and of figure so majestic that his head seemed to touch the clouds.

The blessed man having announced his name to the king, stood in the midst of the camp, and covered it all with his brilliant garment, except at one small distant point; and at the same time he uttered those cheering words which the Lord spake to [Joshua] Ben Nun before the passage of the Jordan, after Moses' death, saying, "Be strong and of a good courage; behold, I shall be with thee," etc.

Then St. Columba having said these words to the king in the vision, added, "March out this following night from your camp to battle, for on this occasion the Lord has granted to me that your foes shall be put to flight, that your enemy [Cadwallon] shall be delivered into your hands, and that after the battle you shall return in triumph, and have a happy reign."

(trans. William Reeves, 1874)

Here we can see the Celtic abbot Adamnan using a technique familiar to readers of Bede. By invoking Joshua, he is trying to draw a comparison between this Old Testament figure and what was to him a fairly modern one: in fact later in his biography of St Columba Adamnan tells us that had this narrative 'from the lips of my predecessor, the Abbot Failbe, who solemnly declared that he had himself heard King Oswald relating this same vision to Segine the abbot'.

For Joshua crossing the Jordan, see Joshua 3: it is interesting that in this chapter from the Old Testament, the Ark of the Covenant serves a similar purpose to Oswald's cross at Heavenfield, and also the Christian symbols painted on the shields of Constantine's troops at the Battle of the Milvian Bridge. The Cathach of St Columba, a partial psalter or book of psalms supposedly written out by the saint, was also used as a lucky charm in battle, and an exquisite 'folded' gold cross, the heaviest object from the Staffordshire Hoard, was almost certainly designed to be used as a battle-standard. Note that Adamnan also has Columba telling Oswald who he is: the saint had been dead for some years before Oswald was born, so the Anglo-Saxon prince would not necessarily have recognised him.

Bede attributes Oswald's victory at Heavenfield to heavenly intervention, but some readers might be happier with a more down-to-earth explanation. It may be that Oswald's Anglo-Saxons were able to beat Cadwallon's larger force of Britons simply because the English were better fighters. As he saw his army disintegrating before the Saxons' advance, Cadwallon may have sighed and remembered how time after time, over centuries, the Saxons had tended to get the better of the British in battles on British soil. This was how the Saxons had managed to overrun much of Great Britain, turning the British into second-class citizens or refugees in their own land, and forming a new ruling class of petty Saxon kings.

The Saxon aptitude for war was probably both genetic and cultural. The ancestors of Saxons like Oswald had been drafted in by the Britons as mercenaries to fight off invasions of Picts from the north, and sea-borne raiders from Ireland. The Britons needed military help because early in the fifth century the last Roman legionaries had withdrawn from their shores. Bede tells us that the hard-pressed Britons wrote to Rome, complaining that 'the barbarians drive us to the sea; the sea drives us back to the barbarians: between them we are exposed to two sorts of death; we are either slaughtered or drowned', but the Romans themselves were hard-pressed at the time, and could offer no further assistance.

The British king Vortigern is supposed to have invited the Saxons to settle in his country, at some point in the middle of the fifth century, on condition that they fought the Picts for him. But the new arrivals turned on their masters, made a pact with the Picts, and began to dominate their new home. The Saxons, as Bede writes:

. . . ravaged all the neighbouring cities and country, spread the conflagration from the eastern to the western sea, without any opposition, and overran the whole face of the doomed island. Public as well as private buildings were overturned; the priests were everywhere slain before the altars; no respect was shown for office, the prelates with the people were destroyed with fire and sword; nor were there any left to bury those who had been thus cruelly slaughtered. Some of the miserable remnant, being taken in the mountains, were butchered in heaps. Others, spent with hunger, came forth and submitted themselves to the enemy, to undergo for the sake of food perpetual servitude, if they were not killed upon the spot. Some, with sorrowful hearts, fled beyond the seas. Others, remaining in their own country, led a miserable life of terror and anxiety of mind among the mountains, woods and crags.

It was easy for Bede the Christian to attribute Oswald's victory at Heavenfield to his faith in the symbol of the cross, but how to explain the success of the pagan Saxons against the Christian British, nearly two hundred years earlier? One of the Britons who 'with sorrowful hearts, fled beyond the seas' was the sixth-century monk-chronicler Gildas. Like Bede, the author of *On the Ruin and Conquest of Britain* attributed the 'general destruction of everything that is good, and the general growth of evil throughout the land' to the laziness of his fellow-Britons, their foolish neglect of their Christian religion, their 'diabolical idols', their rebelliousness and their tendency to put sensual pleasure before everything else.

Historians have tried to reconstruct how the Saxons, who ultimately prevailed against the Britons, fought their battles, drawing on written evidence, archaeology, and sources such as the Bayeux Tapestry. It is thought that these Germanic hammers of the native Britons rode to and from their battles on horses, but preferred to fight on foot. Not for them the cavalry charge or the war-chariot. On the Tapestry, some of Harold's soldiers are shown forming a shield-wall. The forming, breaching, breaking and scattering of these shield-walls were major concerns for the warriors of the time.

Behind their wooden shields, reinforced with metal bosses, the Saxons stood, the luckier ones in chain-mail, with metal helmets on their heads. To judge from the celebrated Sutton

Hoo helmet, which now seems to have become a sort of icon for the Saxon age, some of these helmets had masks designed to protect the face.

This famous helmet, and many other gorgeous, gold- or silver-plated, bejewelled Anglo-Saxon accoutrements of war, are known to have been worn in battle, and not just for show, for instance on ceremonial occasions. This undoubtedly made the warriors of the time very impressive to look at, but as the Staffordshire Hoard, discovered in 2009, clearly shows, these treasures were routinely stripped as loot from fallen combatants.

The Staffordshire Hoard, which was discovered in 2009, is the largest hoard of Saxon gold ever found. Many of the items that are now on display at Stoke-on-Trent are horribly twisted or folded, either because they were hastily ripped from a wooden shield or similar mount in the aftermath of a battle, or because they needed to be folded up to fit into a smaller space. The Hoard may date from around the time of Aidan's death in 651, or up to some twenty-five years later.

As opposing shield-walls came closer together, javelins would be thrown and then long spears used to probe the opposing wall, looking for weaknesses. Spear-thrusts from above or below might get behind a shield and find some unprotected flesh. Close-quarters meant that the swords came out. Despite the lack of guns and bombs, the noise must have been terrifying – crunching, clattering, clanging, and of course shouted orders and the cries of the injured and dying. It seems that the twanging of bows and the hiss and thud of arrows were not much heard: this was before the age of the terrifying English longbow.

The ghastly aftermath of such a battle is nicely conveyed in part of Alfred Tennyson's translation of the Anglo-Saxon poem *The Battle of Brunanburgh*:

Many a carcase they left to be carrion,
Many a livid one, many a sallow-skin—
Left for the white-tail'd eagle to tear it, and
Left for the horny-nibb'd raven to rend it, and
Gave to the garbaging war-hawk to gorge it, and
That gray beast, the wolf of the weald.

Bede was writing a century after Oswald's victory, but something that was supposed to be Oswald's cross was still standing at Heavenfield in his day, though pilgrims to the site had a habit of cutting splinters from the cross itself. These they put into water which, when drunk by sick people or ailing cattle, wrought miraculous cures. Even when sufferers were just sprinkled with such water, they got better.

The moss that grew on the old cross could also be efficacious. A monk called Bothelm broke his arm when he fell through some ice, and it seems that it was never properly set. It gave him agony until a fellow-monk gave him a piece of the moss. After he had slept all night with the moss next to his skin, he woke the next morning to find that his arm was completely healed.

The monk with the broken arm was from the abbey at Hexham. The Hexham monks made a pilgrimage to Heavenfield every year on the fourth of August, the day before Oswald is supposed to have been killed in 642. They would keep a vigil for the health of Oswald's soul, sing psalms and perform a Mass. Bede was pleased to note that a chapel had recently been built at Heavenfield: the modest outline of this Saxon building has been discovered, but the current church of Saint Oswald is much later.

II. Sown Among Thorns

As soon as the victorious Oswald assumed the throne of Northumbria, he set about trying to convert his subjects to Christianity. Since he had learned about the faith from the Scots, it was natural for him to asks the Scots to send him one of their bishops, to act as missionary to his pagan Northumbrians. Unfortunately, the first bishop they sent was quite unsuited to the task. Bede tells us very little about this man, and does not even mention his name. By contrast, the sixteenth-century Scottish historian Hector Boece names the bishop, and goes into a lot of detail about his abortive mission.

Boece's unusual surname is a medieval spelling of the name Boethius: that fourth-century Roman philosopher was, as we know, one of the wise souls whom Dante put into the sun, together with Bede, King Solomon and others, in his *Divine Comedy*. In his Latin *History and Chronicles of Scotland*, Hector Boece tells us that the failed missionary's name was Corman, and that, in the words of John Bellenden's translation into Scots, he was 'ane man of na les gravite than erudition' (a man of no less gravity than erudition). Unfortunately Corman's erudition, or impressive learning, was coupled with an intellectual vanity that was not appropriate for a monkish priest in his position, and lent him the 'gravite' that the Saxons evidently found unattractive.

Corman spent a long time with Oswald's people, delivering sermons that were 'so curious' (meaning complex or elaborate) 'that they appeared more for vain ostentation and pride, than any doctrine, to the people'. At last Corman returned to Scotland and declared to an assembly of prelates 'that the Northumbrians were so dull, that no doctrine might profit there'. The Saxons not only refused to do what Corman told them to do, 'but condemned the same, as contrary to their laws and constitutions'.

The assembled prelates were not minded to give up, however, and they 'took sundry considerations, what was best to bring the people out of their errors'. Some thought it would be best to send Corman back, reinforced, this time, with more learned priests. He was, after all, 'right resolute in divine letters, and was a profound clerk'. Surely prolonged hard work would bear fruit, and the result would please their friend, King Oswald? 'Such things might not he hastily done'.

If Corman could not bring it off, said some, then surely there was no point sending missionaries to the Saxons at all? The elders who recommended sending Corman back to Northumbria may have been thinking of Jonah, the Old Testament prophet who refused God's instruction to go on a mission to Nineveh, only to be taken there by force in the belly of a fish.

The elders' keenness to please Oswald by re-launching their missionary effort hints at motivations for Corman's mission that go beyond the Celtic believers' determination to spread the Gospel. This powerful Northumbrian king, who had succeeded in fending off dangerous enemies, had reunited a large territory that was not too far from the Scottish sphere of influence to the north-west. His friendship might be easier to turn into a political and military alliance if his entire kingdom became Christian. It might then be easier to, for instance, arrange dynastic marriages between aristocratic Northumbrians and their equivalents among the Scots.

At this point in Boece's narrative, when the Northumbrian mission might have been kicked into the long grass, 'Aidan the holy bishop' pipes up, and suggests that:

To bring men from errors, and to reduce them to secure faith, I think it expedient, wise fathers, to show such things in the beginning, as may persuade them in fervent love of God; and when the preacher has made the people desirous to hear his sermon, and obtained their benevolence, to preach first the fundamentals of the Christian faith, but without any ostentation or arrogance, not involving the people with such difficult matters as may not be apprehended by them, as the minds of men are not drawn hastily from evil custom, and since they acquire knowledge and virtue by process of time, and learn the simplest matters first.

By this way, I trust their knowledge is the more imprinted in their breasts. Therefore, if the reverend bishop Corman had observed this right in the beginning, and abstained from the curious questions of our faith, I doubt not but the people should have been obedient to his commandments. Therefore, since nothing has been done which King Oswald desired, I think the blame must attach as much to Corman as the people. I think it best to send a new preacher to Northumberland, who will first, in his preaching, give them milk, and after, more solid food. Otherwise, they will never be brought to the faith.

Anyone who has ever attended more than a handful of committees or other business meetings will recognise what happened next. All eyes turned to Aidan. He had just volunteered himself as Corman's replacement.

The story has many interesting aspects, and one can hardly blame Hector Boece for elaborating it, probably beyond anything he found in its sources. As presented by the Scotsman, the tale is a warning against intellectual vanity, and a reminder of the complex relationship that exists between the content of a message and its means of delivery. According to the title of an important 1967 book by the Canadian theorist Marshall McCluhan, 'the medium is the message'. We can imagine how this would have played out in the context of Oswald's Northumbria. To some of the Northumbrian courtiers, Corman not only *represented* Christianity, he *was* Christianity. If he gave the impression that Christianity was both both complex and arrogant, that was bound to put them off.

By starting the Northumbrian pagans on the milk of easier ideas, then weaning them off on to something more substantial, Aidan was not falsifying the Christian message, but carefully curating it. He set off for Oswald's court hoping to find the right message to fit his task of preaching to a particular set of people in a particular place and time.

By using the simile of weaning in his speech before the elders, Aidan was also representing the business of Christian teaching as something entirely natural and wholesome. The simile, which Boece probably got direct from Bede's *Ecclesiastical History*, also conceals an ambiguity at the heart of the story, as presented by Bede himself. Were Colman's sermons harsh because they were intellectually challenging, or because they were terrifying 'hellfire' sermons, threatening the spiritual stick of Hell rather than offering the carrot of Heaven? Perhaps they were both curious and scary. Given the asceticism or deliberate hard-living of many of the Irish monks, it may be that Corman was suggesting that fasting, sleeplessness and general mortification of the flesh were the only ways to Heaven. This also might have seemed off-putting at first.

The story of Corman's replacement by Aidan also sets up a striking contrast between the two men. While Corman is negative, dismissing the Northumbrians as 'dull', Aidan is positive, foregrounding love as the heart of the Christian message. While Corman blames the Northumbrians for his failure, Aidan is not afraid to be more even-handed, even though this might be taken as an insult by a fellow priest: Corman must also take some of the blame. Corman is complex, while Aidan favours simplicity. Corman is arrogant, but Aidan is humble.

By having something to say about the delivery of the Christian message, Aidan was also imitating Christ, who was asked by his disciples about his own approach at Mark 4:10. Jesus explained that he spoke in parables because whereas they, the disciples, could understand 'the mysteries of the kingdom of heaven', the people could not; 'for this people's heart is waxed gross, and their ears are dull of hearing, and their eyes they have closed' (Mark 4:15). Corman might have agreed with Jesus about the dullness of the people, but both Jesus and Aidan wanted to wake the people up, and restore their spiritual senses.

In the Gospel of Mark, the disciples' question to Jesus, about his use of parables, comes after his powerful parable of the sower. Here the message, or the kingdom of God, is compared to seed that is widely sown, but the crop only grows well on 'good ground' where it 'sprang up and increased, and brought forth, some thirty, and some sixty, and some a hundred' (Mark 4:8). In the terms of this parable, Corman evidently thought that he had sown his corn on 'the wayside, and the fowls of the air came and devoured it up' (Mark 4:4) or 'among thorns, and the thorns grew up, and choked it, and it yielded no fruit' (Mark 4:7). By contrast, Aidan felt that Corman had tried to sow the wrong seeds on the wrong kind of land. Something similar would happen years later, when Cuthbert, a saint who, as we shall see, was inspired by the example of Aidan, tried to grow literal wheat on the bleak, windswept island of Farne. It did not take, but barley did.

Corman might have argued that his rejection of Oswald's Angles as proselytes was entirely biblical. Jesus' advice to his disciples at Matthew 10:14 is to travel around offering their message; but he adds: 'whosoever shall not receive you, nor hear your words, when ye depart out of that house or city, shake off the dust of your feet'. This was a piece of deliberate body-language used at the time, which said, 'you won't be seeing me again'. Aidan's predecessor as preacher to Oswald's court was shaking the metaphorical dust from his feet after having tried to make the Northumbrians hear his words for some time. Aidan's advice was not to abandon the reluctant hearers forever, but to return and try again, or send someone else with a new approach.

We might characterise Aidan's attitude as originating in a generous, positive feeling about the supposedly 'dull' Northumbrians who had refused to listen to Corman. Corman may have thought Aidan was being a bit of a Polyanna, centuries before that boundlessly optimistic character was invented by the American novelist Eleanor Porter. Jesus was clear that when his disciples shook the dust from their feet outside a house, 'it shall be more tolerable for the land of

Sodom and Gomorrha in the day of judgment, than for that city' (Matthew 10:15). The parable of the sower also implies that the human equivalents of the stony ground and the thorny ground are unable, by their nature, to accept the word. Aidan, by contrast, wanted to clear the stones out of the metaphorical stony ground, and pull up the thorns, to give the seed a better chance.

Although it was probably against Aidan's own character to dismiss an entire ethnic group as 'dull', Corman was certainly not the first or the last to cast shade on the culture of the Germanic peoples, from whom Oswald's Angles were an off-shoot.

In his *Germania*, written about a hundred years after the birth of Christ, the Roman historian Tacitus voiced his admiration for the martial spirit of the Anglo-Saxons' Germanic ancestors, but also took exception to their laziness, their drunkenness, and the disinclination of the younger men in particular to do anything other than fight. This meant, among other things, that the fertile lands controlled by the German tribes were shamefully neglected in Tacitus' time.

Bede himself objected to the behaviour of one of his countrymen in his letter to Bishop Egbert of York, of which we have heard before, written near the end of the chronicler's life, in 734. In the letter, Bede advises his correspondent to avoid idle get-togethers where himself and his drunken, over-fed companions might indulge in loose gossip. If nothing else, he implies, such behaviour is bound to leave a bishop with much less time to earn his salt by touring around his diocese spreading the word, even to the poorest and most remote villages. Bede also reminds Egbert of wealthy so-called monasteries, the leaders of which 'do nothing therein but gratify their desires' (trans. J.A. Giles, 1843). The chronicler fears that the amount of land controlled by the church has created a generation of landless men whose behaviour is out of control: these people think nothing of fighting in the armies of England's enemies, and even raping nuns.

Over sixty years after Bede's correspondence with Bishop Egbert, the English priest and scholar Alcuin wrote a similarly critical letter to a bishop living in the kingdom of Mercia, complaining about the terrific banquets that he held, where the prelate and many unsuitable and over-dressed guests, including 'entertainers', would stuff themselves with food, get roaring drunk, listen to harp-music and, worst of all, hear stories about pagan heroes like Ingeld, a character who appears in the anonymous Anglo-Saxon poem *Beowulf*.

As he died in 804, Alcuin may not have known about *Beowulf* itself, or at least not in the form in which we know it, which probably dates from the late tenth or early eleventh centuries. The *Beowulf* that has been endlessly translated (there are at least eight versions in Japanese alone), adapted for radio and films, and studied by generations of students of English Literature, is full of references to the Christian god, but it is unlikely that Alcuin would have approved of it any more than he approved of that lost pagan epic about Ingeld.

Beowulf, which is perhaps the most spectacular artefact left to us by the Anglo-Saxons, is evidently a Christian adaptation of an old pagan legend that had circulated for centuries in the oral tradition. The action involves real historical characters from sixth-century Scandinavia who are also known from other sources, and although on one level *Beowulf* is a simple tale of a man who fights monsters, the elaborate structure and technicolour language give an impression of vividness, profound depth and emotional subtlety.

Alcuin might have objected that the poem still implies that to live well a man must be a reckless, hard-drinking warrior; but perhaps he would also have noticed how the anonymous poet also lays bare the bleakness of lives lived in armour, in almost exclusively male company, in the days when any night might herald yet another raid mounted by the enemy, whether a monster, a foreign invader or a treacherous relative.

Anyone who reads and understands *Beowulf* properly cannot hold on to the idea that the Anglo-Saxons were all coarse, crude and boorish. If nothing else, the historical Scandinavian setting of the poem shows that the English culture that produced the prodigiously talented *Beowulf* poet had international connections and a sense of its own history and origins. The poem's lovingly detailed descriptions of the accoutrements of war and of other treasures remind one irresistibly of some of the stunning objects found in the Sutton Hoo ship burial. This discovery laid bare the wealth and sophistication of the culture that had produced it. The intricate designs that embellish some of the artefacts, with their sinuous, interlocking shapes, beguile and baffle the eye, yet the objects are also entirely practical and suited to their function.

The impression of depth created by some of these designs is reminiscent of the structure of *Beowulf*: the story seems to emerge out an endless web of other stories. Mini-stories are embedded in the poem, in much the same way that precious, exotic stones are embedded in the gold of some of the Sutton Hoo objects. Some of these stones have other stones embedded in them in turn, creating an impression similar to the effect of perspective in some Renaissance paintings.

The knotted, sinuous forms of Anglo-Saxon art, which are similar to those that are characteristic of Celtic art and design, were used to great effect in Christian illuminated manuscripts such as the sixth-century Lindisfarne Gospels, the Book of Durrow and the Book of Kells.

Some of the items found at Sutton Hoo were not locally made, but originated in far-flung places such as Egypt, and the Byzantine or Eastern Roman empire, then ruled from Constantinople. Some of the garnets that were incorporated by local craftsmen into some of the locally-made objects came from Sri Lanka, and all of the coins were from the empire of the Franks, which then stretched across large areas of modern France and Germany.

Even the solidified fragments of bitumen that were scattered among the treasures were found to have originated in the Middle East, after chemical analysis conducted in 2016. These are the dried-up remains of a tarry substance used to waterproof the buried ship in which the treasures were found. That the Anglo-Saxon kingdoms somehow maintained trade-links with such distant places does not indicate an insular, ignorant culture. The design of the Sutton Hoo ship itself, which had sailed the seas before it was buried as a sort of giant nautical coffin, was robust, practical and elegant. At nearly ninety feet, it was somewhat longer than a regulation tennis-court.

Whether the Northumbrians were dull or not, the Scottish missionaries were asking a lot of them, expecting them to abandon their ancient religion and adopt something that must have seemed strange and foreign. They knew who Woden was – he was a direct ancestor of some of them, or so they thought. But who was Jesus, this holy man from a distant, dry, hot country that they could hardly imagine? Weren't gods supposed to bring wealth? Why were Jesus and his followers poor? The old gods had offspring, they had sex and fought battles like mortal people. Where were Jesus's wife and children, and why did his followers favour celibacy? If Jesus was God's son, were they both gods; or is there only one God? If these Scottish monks set such store by their sacred books, how can we become Christians when we can't read a word? Do we have to learn Latin to become Christians?

The Anglo-Saxon Heptarchy (1914)

Map of Iona or 'Hy'

Detail of painting of Bamburgh by John Varley, 1827 (NY Met Museum)

Detail of eighteenth-century painting of Lindisfarne
by Thomas Girtin (NY Met)

U.S. stained glass Aidan (pic. by Randy Greve)

Anglo-Saxon brooch (NY Met)

St Cuthbert, from a twelfth century MS (BL)

Statue of Aidan on Lindisfarne (pic.. by Tony Buglass)

III. The Good Seed

Some of Oswald's followers may have found the transition from paganism to Christianity easier than we might think, because of the similarities between their Germanic form of paganism and certain aspects of Christianity. There were, after all, pagan priests, as there were Christian ones, and pagan temples that preceded the later Christian churches. While the Christians had their holy books, the Germanic pagans had an oral tradition that was rich in myth, legend, symbolism, tradition, poetry and prophecy.

Places that had been sacred to pagan gods before Christianity took root often became associated with local Christian saints. All over Christian Europe, churches and chapels were being built on the sites of old pagan places of worship. While Christians who revered St Oswald may have made sense of him by, as we have seen, giving him some of the attributes of Woden, myths about Woden might also have helped them understand Jesus as well. While Jesus died nailed to a cross, Woden hung from a tree called Yggdrasil for nine days. Both Jesus and Woden were stabbed with spears while they hung on their respective trees. Woden's tree, Yggdrasil, was supposed to be an ash, as was the tree on which Oswald's arm was hung, after his death, by a raven.

Woden, Oswald and Jesus are all associated with the number twelve. Jesus had twelve disciples, and Woden's closest associates were twelve chiefs. Some sources say that Oswald returned from exile with twelve friends who had all been baptised into the Christian faith, as he had been. Both Jesus and Woden could bring dead people back to life, and in a German account of Oswald's life, the holy king revives the dead bodies of his enemy's fallen soldiers. Jesus and Woden appeared to people after their deaths, Woden often turning up on the eve of a battle to give encouragement to the leader of one side. As we have seen, St Columba, the founder of the monastery on Iona, appeared to Oswald in a dream before the Battle of Heavenfield. Columba is also supposed to have arrived for the first time on Iona with twelve followers, although he may have chosen this number in imitation of Jesus and his disciples.

For some of Aidan's hearers, the leap of faith into the new system of belief would not have been a very long jump at all, not just because they could see the similarities between the old and new religions, but also because they were already familiar with Christianity. There were Oswald's twelve baptised companions, and some of the older courtiers may have been veterans of the court of the earlier Northumbrian king Edwin, who, as we know, had himself become Christian, after much agonising and discussion. Some may have visited, or met and spoken to visitors from, the lands of the Christian Celts, or the kingdoms where some of their own people, the Anglo-Saxons, had already embraced Christianity.

Aidan arrived in Northumbria less than forty years after another Christian mission, led by St Augustine of Canterbury, had arrived on the island of Thanet, off the coast of Kent, in 597. Augustine and his followers, who may have numbered about forty, had been sent by Pope Gregory the Great, who had been dreaming of Christianising the pagan English for some time. The legend, as related by Bede, is that at some point before he himself became pope in 590, Gregory saw a couple of English boys for sale in a slave market in Rome (although another version of the story states that they were free visitors to the Eternal City). Struck by their pale beauty, he asked where they were from. 'They are Angles,' came the reply. Gregory indulged in a pun, implying that the boys looked like angels. When he learned that the came from Deira, he expressed a hope that they might avoid the wrath (*ira*) of God. Since their king was Aella, he hoped that the Angles might learn to sing alleluias. After this encounter, Gregory began to plan the conversion of the English pagans.

Gregory would have preferred to lead a mission to the Angles in person, but he was considered such an asset in Rome that both pope and people were alarmed by the prospect of his departure. He actually set off on the long journey to Britain, but was fetched back. By this time he believed he had already been shown a sign from God, telling him to make a u-turn. He had seen a locust, and the Latin word for that insect reminded his punning brain of the Latin for 'stay put'.

As pope, Gregory earned the title 'the Great' by being very energetic, and forcefully asserting the authority of the papacy. Gregory, who has been described as the first medieval pope, expended a lot of his energy on suppressing paganism, and what he regarded as Christian heresy. This was long before the Great Schism of the eleventh century, when the Catholic and Orthodox churches separated. Gregory believed that as bishop of Rome he had authority over such figures as the Greek-speaking prelates of Byzantium.

Readers should not imagine that the Rome where Gregory lived, not on the Vatican but on the Lateran hill, was the thriving, glittering city that it had been under the greatest of the Caesars. It had been hammered by invasions, and was threatened by the ominous presence of the Lombards on Italian soil. Like the Anglo-Saxons, the Lombards were a Germanic people, and in Gregory's day many of them were Christian heretics, following the Arian way.

In his book *Crises in the History of the Papacy*, Joseph McCabe describes the chaotic, decayed city in which Pope Gregory lived and worked:

across the Tiber from the old quarter, there were to be seen only the mouldering crowns of the theatres and amphitheatres, the grass-girt ruins on the Capitol and on the Palatine, and the charred skeletons of thousands of patrician mansions on the more distant hills. Forty thousand Romans now trembled where a million had once boasted their eternal empire.

McCabe's picture turns even darker when he reminds us that Pope Gregory's Rome was regularly affected by devastating plagues and famines.

In theory, Rome should have been able to depend on help from the eastern wing of the Roman Empire, but in practice the Byzantine emperors, based in Constantinople, had their hands full with their own problems. Gregory, a natural leader and an eminently practical man with an astounding eye for detail, attempted to fill this power-vacuum, asserting papal authority via skilful diplomacy and, on occasion, military force.

Although he worked hard and successfully to maximise his income from the Church's widespread assets, this powerful pope continued to live a life of bleak asceticism, wrecking his health with extreme fasts and sleep-deprivation. Not for him the decadent life-styles he had seen among the million or so people who lived at Constantinople, the new secular capital of the Roman world. The diminutive size of his own personal expenditure was part of what allowed him to relieve the distress of his fellow-Romans in the west with charitable donations, particularly of food.

Augustine, whom Gregory sent to the Angles, had been prior of a monastery in Rome. He first met the Kentish king Ethelbert on Thanet. Ethelbert should not, of course, be confused with Ethelfrith, the Northumbrian king who was Oswald's father, and ruled in the north at the same time Ethelbert ruled in Kent. Augustine's mission came equipped with Frankish interpreters: a typically practical idea that had been suggested to them by Pope Gregory. Gregory had evidently made such constant use of interpreters himself during the years he spent at Constantinople that he failed to learn a word of Greek.

King Ethelbert's influence stretched well beyond Kent itself, and Bede tells us that 'he had extended his dominions as far as the boundary formed by the great river Humber, by which the Southern Saxons are divided from the Northern'. He was not a complete stranger to Christianity since his wife, Bertha, was a Christian Frank. Nevertheless it seems that the Kentish king suspected that Augustine and his followers might be sorcerers of some kind, and he insisted on meeting them first in the open air, where he thought their magic, if they had any, might have less power against him.

Augustine's mission to Kent is the reason why Canterbury has long been such an important place for English Christians, and why, after the Queen, the archbishop of Canterbury is the most powerful figure in the Anglican Church. This was the form of Christianity that King Readwald of the East Angles mixed with paganism, and which Oswald's uncle Edwin learned about during his exile at Readwald's court. As we know, Edwin did not convert until he was king of Northumbria.

Augustine's faith was different from the Celtic Christianity preached by Aidan, though the doctrinal differences between these two strands of Christianity have sometimes been exaggerated. One crucial difference was that Augustine's message had the backing of a successor of St Peter, who lived in a city where some of the earliest Christians had lived, worshipping in secret in the catacombs and elsewhere. This was also the city where Peter, the rock on whom Jesus said he would build his church, was probably crucified, on the Vatican hill that would later become the home of his successors. St Paul of Tarsus also knew Rome, and wrote one of his celebrated letters to the Christians there. This was also the city where the pagan emperor Nero used burning Christian martyrs as giant candles.

Hector Boece tells us that shortly after Aidan arrived at the court of King Oswald, as Corman's replacement, his message began to take off in a phenomenal way. 'At his coming', Hector writes:

. . . so many people came the hear him, that he was forced to preach outside the churches, because of the sheer numbers of people who wanted to hear him preach. Because Aidan did not know the language of the Saxons, preaching was a problem for him, but King Oswald knew both the Scottish and the Saxon languages, and could translate Aidan's sermons for the people. Their words were held in great veneration, and seven thousand Saxons were converted to the Christian faith in just a few days. In those days, the Saxons were called the English. The Northumbrians chose Aidan to be their bishop, and because their devotion increased every day, and every day new priests arrived to support Aidan, many new churches were built in Northumbria, and dedicated to God and the Virgin Mary. In this way, the region became no less Catholic than any other province of England.

Bede tells us that it was a beautiful sight 'to see the king himself interpreting the Word of God to his ealdormen and thegns, for he had thoroughly learned the language of the Scots during his long banishment'.

Bede assures us that part of the process of converting Northumbria to Christianity was the ordination of many Saxon men into the priesthood, and the adoption of Saxon monks. This would have involved considerable sacrifices for the men involved, especially if they were young men who had previously expected to live out their lives as hard-drinking warriors, feasting at their king's table and enjoying female companionship. Aidan's monks swapped the prospect of a wife and family for the companionship of their brother monks; rich food and drink for frugal teetotal dinners; and immersion in the oral tradition of pagan legends for the Bible and the writings of the Church Fathers.

In embracing the cloistered life Aidan's Saxon recruits would, however, have won approval from their king, and their education as monks would have allowed them to wean themselves off the milk of their bishop's initial preaching and onto the solid food of theology, and the assimilation of new languages – particularly Irish and Latin. For some people, learning, motivated by curiosity, is a reward in itself. Huddled over a book in a hut on an island in the North Sea, Aidan's Saxon monks could take their first steps into a wider world; the world of the shores of, and the islands in, the Mediterranean; of Rome, Greece, Egypt and the Holy Land.

By embracing the monastic life the new Saxon monks would also have been renouncing the horrors of the battlefield – the screams of the injured and dying, the stench of blood and the possibility of an early death, or disgrace as a coward, or life with a maimed body or broken mind.

One would think that, as a monk himself, Bede would have approved of the idea of large numbers of Saxons taking up the cloistered life. But by the time he wrote his Letter to Egbert, nearly a century after Aidan arrived in Northumbria, so many young men had gone into monasteries that Bede was concerned that there were not enough of them left to defend the Anglo-Saxon kingdoms. The chronicler also told Egbert that if so much land was given over to monasteries, there might not be enough to give to military veterans, to reward them for their service and encourage them to settle down after a lifetime of fighting. These landless veterans were the people Bede feared might end up fighting for England's enemies, abandoning all sense of loyalty and morality, and even resorting to raping nuns.

By the 730s, it seems, many of the monasteries that had been set up were not, according to Bede's standards, being run according to any acceptable monastic rule, and were just places where lazy people could indulge themselves. In his letter, Bede insists that Egbert, as a bishop, should do everything he can to reform such places; to turn them 'from luxury to chastity, from vanity to verity, from indulgence of the stomach and the gullet to continence and heartfelt piety' (trans. McClure and Collins, 1994).

Although, as his Letter to Egbert shows, Bede could be very critical of some of the forms of monasticism that existed in his own time, it is important to note that he was not critical of the monasticism Aidan had introduced into Northumbria a century earlier. Laudable as it no doubt was in many ways, the new way of life that Celtic Christianity was offering to Oswald's people represented a big change.

Later we will meet 'Fifel': this is the name given to the skeleton of an elderly man who was recently discovered buried at Bowl Hole near Bamburgh. Analysis of his teeth has revealed that he originally came from what we now call western Scotland, and it seems that at some point he may have broken some ribs, perhaps in a battle.

In some imaginary novel based on the life of this man, we can visualise a chapter where the hero questions his son about his monastic vocation. Coming from a Celtic Christian community where monasticism had long been a fact of life, 'Fifel' the uprooted Scot may have been enthusiastic about the idea. Having seen the horrors of war, and having perhaps been wounded in battle himself, the father might have liked the idea of his precious son embracing a life of peace and contemplation.

But maybe his wife, who was perhaps a local Saxon woman, was not so sanguine: she had problems understanding what monasticism was, wanted her son to be a warrior, and looked forward to the appearance of the grand-children who would have been denied to her by monasticism. This is how historical change impacts ordinary people: new opportunities appear, but old ways of life are suddenly off the table. Young people in particular have to face choices that their parents never faced.

In the passage excerpted above, Hector Boece seems to imply that Aidan became the local bishop because he won the approbation of the people. In fact he was probably already a bishop before he set off to preach to the English, and he was confirmed in this position by King Oswald, not by the Northumbrians in general. As we know, some Irish accounts suggest that he may already have been an abbot and a bishop on Scattery Island in the Shannon estuary. Part of Oswald's royal confirmation comprised the business of giving Aidan and his monks the island of Lindisfarne as the headquarters of their mission.

It would seem that Aidan was more successful than Corman partly because he was a different sort of man, and, as we have seen, was careful to adapt his preaching to make it acceptable to new listeners. The fact that Oswald translated for him must have helped, as must the king's gift of the island of Lindisfarne to his new bishop. It is natural to ask, did Oswald offer to translate for Corman, and did he offer *him* Lindisfarne? If not, why did he offer them for the first time to Aidan? Perhaps, when Corman knocked the dust off his shoes and headed home, Oswald was left to reflect that he had not helped the disgruntled bishop as much as he might have done. By the time Aidan arrived, the Northumbrian king was more ready to go the extra mile, to avoid another embarrassing failure.

It may be, of course, that Oswald *had* offered to translate for Corman, but had found his preaching too 'curious' and difficult to understand. If he could not comprehend it himself, how could he convey its meaning in English? The idea of giving Lindisfarne to Corman and his monks may never have occurred to Oswald, and Corman's sense of the dullness of the Saxons may have been reinforced by his having to live cheek by jowl with Oswald's courtiers, instead of at a convenient distance.

An important centre of Oswald's kingdom was Bamburgh, a fortress on a rock, the base of which was then washed by the North Sea at high tide. The place is said to have been named after Oswald's step-mother, Queen Bebba. The rock on which the fortress stood rises like a bison's hunched back out of the coastal landscape. The rock itself is a steep-sided 'sill' of dolerite, a hard grey volcanic rock. It is a section of the Great Whin Sill: other parts of the formation can be seen at Dunstanburgh Castle, Hadrian's Wall and the High Force waterfall in Teesdale. Presumably King Oswald would have ordered that the steep rocks that loomed below his ramparts should always be kept clear of vegetation, which could have concealed enemies trying to climb up, and given them something to hold on to as they climbed.

The Bamburgh sill has been occupied by humans for at least two thousand years. It must have been recognised by the iron-age people who first claimed it as an easily-defensible site and a good lookout point from which to see threats approaching by land or sea. Modern visitors see stone walls, a castle and other structures here, including the remains of an old windmill, but in Aidan's time the top of the rock would have been host to a scatter of wooden buildings, probably defended by a box-rampart. This would have comprised two wooden walls, one inside the other, the gap being filled with rocks and rubble. A wooden walkway would have been built over the in-fill, for the lookouts who patrolled the walls.

There were at least two wells inside the ramparts, so that during a siege the besieged would not die of thirst. One of these had been dug by repeatedly heating the rock with fire, then dousing it with cold water so that it shattered and became easier to move. The time and trouble were worth it: sieges were won or lost because of the issue of drinking-water.

To withstand a siege of any length, the Bamburgh settlement would have needed some way to store a supply of food that was able to last for at least a few weeks. The demands on this food may have increased if locals from outside the fortress moved there for protection, having heard of the approach of the enemy. Given the technology of the time, emergency rations might have consisted of the contents of a good dry granary. To turn the corn into something edible, such as bread, or pottage, a type of savoury porridge, a stock-pile of fuel would also have been needed. Oswald's Bamburgh must also have had an arsenal of some kind as well.

An attempt to besiege such a fortress is depicted on the lid of the so-called Franks Casket, an elaborately-carved Anglo-Saxon whalebone box from the eighth century. Here the besiegers with their small round shields, spears, swords and chain-mail are being showered with arrows from the ramparts, which are topped with triangular crenellations like wooden sharks' teeth. Some of the aggressors have fallen under the walls of the fortress, while others are finding that their bucklers are not impervious to arrows. The Franks Casket can be seen at the British Museum.

The buildings at Bamburgh that the ramparts protected would have included at least one church, kitchens, workshops, and a large hall. Here in the Anglo-Saxon equivalent of the banqueting hall of a later medieval castle, we can imagine scenes unfolding that would remind time-travelling bookworms of those seen in Heorot, the great hall of the Danish king Hrothgar in *Beowulf*. Seated on long wooden benches, guests would stuff themselves with rich food, engage in epic drinking-bouts, brag about their exploits in battle, listen to music, sing songs and hear re-tellings of legends of, perhaps, Ingeld, Woden, and even Beowulf himself.

On the morning after such a gaudy night, Oswald's hung-over followers may indeed have appeared 'dull' if Corman had attempted to interest them in obscure points of theology. Tetchy and in need of a swift hair-of-the-dog, they might also have been tempted to raise grumpy objections to his teachings, especially if any parts they understood were directed against gluttony, violence, drunkenness, fornication, and worldly riches.

An important part of the goings-on in Anglo-Saxon royal halls, which were often magnificent buildings despite their wooden construction, was the giving of just such worldly riches, in the form of gifts. Particularly brave warriors, honoured visitors and other favoured people would be given all sorts of presents, in special ceremonies featuring flowery speeches. *Beowulf* emphasises the importance of gift-giving in the court etiquette of a king or other magnate. Recent archaeology suggests that at least one of the workshops at Bamburgh would have been capable of turning out sophisticated artefacts, the brilliance of which would have enhanced the reputations of the Northumbrian kings, and strengthened the respect and sense of obligation of their followers.

The medical effects of the rich diet of the royal court, and the quantities of alcohol consumed, were laid bare by analysis of the bones found in a graveyard of Aidan's period, at Bowl Hole, a little to the south of the site of Oswald's fortress. The dig, which ended in 2007, found ninety-one skeletons. Some of these may have been the bones of people who actually witnessed Aidan's first sermons in Northumbria. One effect of their indulgent diet was that many of them had dreadful teeth, even the ones who had died young. They seem to have suffered from a perfect storm of sweetened food and a complete lack of modern toothbrushes. On average they were, however, tall and robust, suggesting that, although some of the adults had been malnourished in childhood, they had enjoyed varied food of good quality in adulthood. Chemical analysis of the (often badly decayed) teeth of the individuals buried at Bowl Hole has revealed that very few of them had grown up locally.

The archaeologists have given Anglo-Saxon names to some of these human remains. 'Frymð' died as an adult woman. She has plaque on her teeth, and her leg-bones show signs of her having spent a lot of time squatting. She was unusually tall, and may have died in childbirth or shortly thereafter: the bones of a new-born baby were found buried close to her. She was British, but not local. 'Fifel', whom we have already met, was an old man who suffered from bad teeth, fused vertebrae and osteoarthritis. As we know, at some point he had broken some ribs, perhaps in battle, but these had healed well. As we have seen, he probably grew up in the west of Scotland.

'Hreycg', a young woman who died in her twenties, had plaque on her teeth, indicating a rich, sugary diet, but other evidence suggests that she was anaemic and may have suffered from scurvy. She was also unusually short: was this genetic, or to do with the poor diet that had left her short of iron and Vitamin C? Like 'Frymð', 'Hreycg' was also British, but had not grown up locally.

'Burgware' had particularly bad teeth, although he or she may only have died in their teens. Early-onset osteoarthritis meant that 'Burgware' was probably lame. Like 'Fifel', 'Burgware' came from the west of Scotland.

Like 'Fifel' and 'Burgware', many of the Bowl Hole people came from far to the north and west of Oswald's kingdom, in Ireland or the west of Scotland. Perhaps the links Oswald had forged through Aidan, and earlier, during his exile, with the Christians of Dalriada meant that there was always a warm welcome for such people wherever Oswald held court, at Bamburgh, at Yeavering to the west, or elsewhere. It may be that some of these outsiders had befriended Oswald and his followers during their exile among the Scots, and hoped to capitalise on their connection by relocating to be near their old Saxon friend, who now became their patron.

An author of historical novels might choose to weave a whole story around the mysterious 'Fifel'. Perhaps his parents had been born in Ireland, but had migrated to what we now call Scotland before 'Fifel' was born. As a young man their son, who may have been about Oswald's age, had met the exiled prince and decided to follow him. Perhaps they met before a battle in Ireland where they were both fighting on the same side: we know that Oswald fought alongside his hosts when he was in exile from Northumbria.

Perhaps 'Fifel' had also fought alongside his Saxon master at Heavenfield, broke some ribs there when two shield-walls clashed, but received excellent medical treatment at Bamburgh. There 'Fifel' fell in love with the Saxon maiden who nursed him and, when she had converted to Christianity, the pair had married. We have already imagined the drama that may have unfolded when their son announced that he was thinking of becoming a monk.

Even if they were not professionally involved in preaching the gospel to the Saxon locals, the new arrivals from Dalriada would have raised the proportion of Christians at Bamburgh, and set an example by living as Christian lay-people. They showed the pagan Saxons that Christianity was not all about monks, although monks played a very important role in the Irish version of the faith. Hard-drinking pagan Saxons with big appetites might have been reassured to see members of Northumbria's new Christian population getting just as over-stuffed, drunk, violent and amorous as they did, on occasion.

While the Saxons had the epic poems they had grown from Germanic and Scandinavian roots, the Celts had their own folklore, and when the language barrier began to grow translucent the Saxons could have begun to marvel at tales of the pagan kings, heroes and giants of the Irish, and the wonders performed by their saints, such as Patrick, Brigid and, closer to their own time, Columba. At least one old Irish tale combines Columba and one of the characters in *The Tain*, an epic tale that could be called the Irish *Beowulf*. When, for bizarre reasons, a group of poets was trying (and failing) to get hold of the story of *The Tain* by interviewing story-tellers who were still following the oral tradition, they turned to Columba for help. The saint resurrected one Fergus Mac Róich, who rose up from his grave and told the whole story, which was then written down on the hide of a cow.

Another story that combines a Christian saint with a character from pagan legend involves St Patrick and Cú Chulainn, the 'Hound of Ulster', the Irish super-hero at the centre of *The Tain*. Patrick is trying to persuade an Irish king to embrace Christianity, but his majesty insists that he will stay pagan unless the saint can bring Cú Chulainn back from the dead. The Hound appears, and assures the king that he has been languishing in hell, and that his majesty should get baptised as soon as possible, to avoid the same fate.

The Tain itself is similar to *Beowulf* in that it has a hero with super-human powers at its centre. Although he is only a teenager, Cú Chulainn is able to bend huge trees into hoops, and behead large numbers of well-armed foes in double-quick time. Even as a small boy, he was able to kill a huge dog just by throwing a ball at it, and he would amuse himself by playing outdoor games, alone against whole teams of older opponents.

The presence of Celtic Christians made Bamburgh and Oswald's other seats multi-cultural and also multi-ethnic. A new generation of half-Scottish, half-Saxon children would soon have begun to appear. Some members of the Northumbrian court would also have had British blood – they may have shared more DNA with the Welsh, far away to the west, than with the Saxons or the Scots. To really thrive in this setting, individuals would have needed an understanding of different cultures, outlooks and religious views. A gift for languages might also have come in very handy.

Christian or pagan, Saxon, Scot or Briton, some of Oswald's companions would not always have been fit company for Aidan and his fellow-monks. It seems that Aidan was reluctant to get too caught up in the rowdy business of dinner *chez* Oswald, and Oswald himself seldom invited him and his monks. Bede tells us that when Aidan was invited, 'which was but seldom . . . he went with one or two clerks, and having taken a little food, made haste to be gone, either to read with his brethren or to pray'.

IV Lindisfarne and Bamburgh

Although Bede tells us that Aidan seldom dined with Oswald, one of the most charming stories involving the two men unfolded during an Easter dinner where both were present. A silver dish 'full of royal dainties' was set before the king, and at that moment 'the servant, whom he had appointed to relieve the needy' rushed in and informed his majesty that 'a great multitude of poor folk from all parts was sitting in the streets begging alms of the king'. Oswald not only had his food sent down to them: he ordered that the silver dish itself be broken up and its pieces distributed among the poor as well. Aidan was so impressed with this apparently spontaneous act of charity that he blessed the king's arm and prayed that it would never decay. The prayer proved to be a prophecy; or we might say that Aidan had lit the fuse on a miracle that would not detonate until some years later.

A full-page illumination in a thirteenth-century manuscript called the Berthold Sacramentary shows this scene, with Oswald in a fine red outfit, handing something that looks more like a gold Easter-egg than a silver dish to a much older-looking Aidan, in a blue bishop's robes and mitre (in fact Aidan was around fourteen years older than Oswald). Lower down the page, we see two scantily-clad paupers making gestures of praise to both king and bishop. Despite the evident age-difference, Aidan and Oswald's faces look like mirror-images of each other: they could be brothers. Both appear to be on the verge of tears: perhaps they both sense that the miraculous preservation of Oswald's generous arm can only happen under grim circumstances.

The story of Oswald's Easter gift is reminiscent of the gift-giving ceremonies that would have happened in Anglo-Saxon mead-halls in both pagan and Christian times, and fulfils some of the traditional functions of gift-giving at the time. Although the spontaneous gift demonstrates his compassion, it also makes it clear that Oswald is wealthy enough to give largely to the poor without making a significant dent in his own wealth, so that in this way his reputation for both wealth and compassion is enhanced.

The involvement in the scene of 'the servant, whom he had appointed to relieve the needy' shows that Oswald's compassion for the poor did not start at that specific Easter Sunday feast. That the king was prepared to give to poor people 'from all parts' suggests that he did not believe that charity should stay at home, but that the royal bounty should stretch even to strangers. That he felt that poverty itself made the poor deserving of charity showed that he had absorbed an important part of the Christian message; he would not give only to those who had served him well, or those with whom he hoped to make a useful alliance.

The story of Oswald and his Easter gesture of charity is reminiscent of the tale told of St Wenceslaus, the tenth-century Bohemian duke (not king) who is immortalised in the Christmas carol *Good King Wenceslaus*. In the carol, Wenceslaus is moved to help the 'poor man' who 'came in sight' not at Easter but on 'the feast of Stephen' after Christmas, when the snow was, of course 'deep and crisp and even'. The duke set off into the 'bitter weather' accompanied by an unnamed page. Together they were able to carry flesh, wine and pine-logs for the poor man's dinner. The pine-logs may have been unnecessary: when they first saw him, the poor man was, after all, 'gathering winter fuel'.

For my taste, the stories of Oswald's Easter charity and Wenceslaus' winter quest both fizzle out unsatisfactorily. Both end with a miracle, but in neither tale do we see the poor objects of charity actually receiving their gifts. How did the poor man in Wenceslaus's story react to a duke arriving on his doorstep laden down with food and drink? What did the poor people at Oswald's door do with their fragments of silver?

That both the English king and the Bohemian duke's festival meals are interrupted is reminiscent of the anonymous English fourteenth-century narrative poem *Sir Gawain and the Green Knight*. Here King Arthur's new year's eve feast at Camelot is not exactly interrupted – by tradition, none of the guests will start to eat until a new adventure has begun. Right on cue, the monstrous Green Knight of the poem's title rides in with a terrifying challenge. Arthur might have been expecting a well-timed delegation of noble ladies dressed in mourning black, begging that one of his knights come and liberate their kingdom, currently enslaved by a dragon; but instead he got a weird green knight.

It is likely that Aidan and his 'clerks' had some sort of base at Bamburgh where they could read or pray when they had skipped out from dinner in Oswald's mead hall. They had the church there of course, but their real home was in their newly-built monastery on the semi-island of Lindisfarne.

Bamburgh and Lindisfarne, which is also known as Holy Island, are a little over five miles apart, and on a good day they have a clear view of each other. Lindisfarne is a semi-island because, as Bede tells us, it 'is twice a day enclosed by the waves of the sea like an island; and again, twice, when the beach is left dry, becomes contiguous with the land'. Geographers call this type of island a tombolo. Today low tide reveals a causeway running from the island, and flat, damp sands that, with great care, can be crossed on foot. In Aidan's day, crossings at high tide could only have been made by boat, and in some weathers this would not have been advisable. At low or high tide, a boat could have crossed straight from Lindisfarne to Bamburgh, in good weather: modern motorists have to add several miles to their journey by crossing to the mainland via the causeway, turning a sharp left, then following the coast-road south.

Whoever came up with the idea of giving Aidan and his monks the island of Lindisfarne as a site for their monastery, it was a stroke of genius. In dangerous times, the monks could cross to Bamburgh to take refuge inside the ramparts, and, in clear weather, lookouts at Bamburgh could spot potential trouble on the island. Messengers and visitors could pass between the two places without much trouble, but days could go by without any contact at all, so that the monks would not weary of the royal court, and the court need not grow weary of the monks. The fact that, with care, the sands that appeared at low tide could be crossed even in certain types of bad weather meant that the monks would not often be completely cut off.

The separation of Aidan and Oswald, the king in his fortress and the bishop on his island, reflected aspects of their status as people. Although Oswald would have felt himself entitled to think of the occupants of Bamburgh and his other palaces as 'his' people, owing loyalty to him and his family, the ultimate loyalty of Aidan and his monks would have been to God. Under certain circumstances, for instance when there was a disagreement between king and bishop, Aidan may have called for help and advice from his own monks on Lindisfarne, from the scriptures or other holy writings, or from colleagues far away on Iona or elsewhere in Dalriada.

Courtiers working directly under King Oswald might have been accused of treason if they had referred their problems to other secular rulers. If one of Oswald's 'ealdormen' or 'thegns' had such a serious disagreement with the king that he felt obliged to stalk out, he would have nowhere to go except perhaps for the court of a rival king. Aidan, by contrast, could have retreated back to Iona, or the Irish mainland, where he would have been out of Oswald's reach and under the protection of the rulers of the separate kingdom of Dalriada.

It is likely that the escape-routes and alternative points of view and sources of help available to royal brides at this time helped their marriages in the same way that Aidan's relative independence helped his relationships with Oswald, and the kings who succeeded him. If the marriage was being wrecked by the bridegroom's controlling behaviour, his bride, who was most likely a princess from a neighbouring kingdom or even a foreign country, could flee back home or call on help from her husband's powerful in-laws. Such royal brides often brought large numbers of followers with them when they moved in with their husbands, including relatives and chaplains.

Oswald might have expected Aidan to confer directly with him on certain matters, but for their working relationship, and their personal relationship, to work, Aidan must have made it clear to his majesty that when it came to some religious matters, and practical matters such as the organisation of his monastery, Oswald's word could not always be the final word. One can imagine a simple Venn diagram of the two men's areas of responsibility, with two circles overlapping in the middle. When this early example of the separation of church and state was working correctly, Oswald and Aidan would only have had to communicate on matters that fell within the overlap.

Bede assures us that Aidan was very bold in speaking truth to power, and pointing out offences and errors. Presumably this boldness would have allowed the bishop to have some productively free and frank discussions with his monarch on matters where their spheres of responsibility, authority and competence overlapped, when such discussions were needed.

For much of the Middle Ages, relationships between monarchs and other aristocrats on the one hand, and children of the Church on the other, were made easier because of the aristocratic backgrounds of the latter. If Bishop Egbert of York had ever taken Bede's advice and called on King Ceolwulf of Northumbria for help, help might have been more forthcoming because Ceolwulf and Egbert were cousins.

According to an 1872 book called *Kalendars of Scottish Saints*, edited by A.P. Forbes, some old Irish sources suggest that St Aidan may have been descended from Eochaidh Finn, a high king of Ireland who may have ruled around the time of the birth of Jesus. Eochaidh was the father of the woman known to the English as Queen Maeve, the formidable warrior-queen who is a leading character in *The Tain*, the great Irish epic. Whether there was a real link between Aidan and these semi-legendary royals, the bishop is supposed to have been able to trace his family back through six generations.

An empire-building Englishman of the nineteenth-century might have dismissed these claims of Irish aristocratic ancestry with a condescending sneer, but as a man who had lived among the Celts, and even learned their language and fought alongside them in battle, Oswald would surely have taken Aidan's antecedents more seriously; if Aidan had ever brushed aside his natural modesty long enough to mention them.

When they were not visiting Bamburgh or the other royal seats of Northumbria, Aidan and his monks probably found Lindisfarne congenial because they were used to islands. For years, Celtic monks and other devoted Christians had been seeking out lonely places, either to live as solitary hermits, or in some kind of community. They were self-consciously copying the example of the first Christian hermits: people like St Anthony of Egypt and St Paul of Thebes, both of whom were Egyptians. Although he lived alone at first, Anthony's way of life proved so enticing that he ended up surrounded by imitators, and eventually became their abbot.

Whereas the Egyptians sought out desert caves, the Celtic Christians were drawn to islands in the sea. One might think that they would plan ahead, ask around about likely islands, then head for one that they had picked in advance, but it is possible that even Columba, the founder of the monastery on Iona, did not do this. Adamnan, his biographer, describes him trying out island after island until he found one from which he could not see Ireland. Adamnan also tells us about the monk Cormac, 'grandson of Lethan' who tried three times to find an island retreat by setting out in a small boat with a party of monks, and allowing God to do the navigating. Columba believed that he failed because one of the monks in his party had not obtained the permission of his abbot to join Cormac's expedition.

Similar problems prolonged Brendan's voyage to the Island of Paradise. Brendan, an Irish saint and older contemporary of Columba, foolishly allowed three extra monks to accompany him on his trip. The result was that he was at sea with his fellow-monks for several years, visiting various strange islands, enduring many bizarre adventures and encountering strange people and mythical creatures. Brendan was only allowed to return home after his three extra passengers had left his ship, by various means.

Later, in 891, the Anglo-Saxon Chronicle records that a party of three Scottish monks; Dubslane, Macbeth and Maelinmun, arrived on the coast of Cornwall in a small currach, a wicker boat waterproofed with hides. They had set off without oars, but with supplies for seven days, hoping that God would guide them to their own island retreat. Having found themselves, instead, in Cornwall, they threw themselves on the mercy of the then English king, Alfred the Great.

This habit of the Celtic monks, their tendency to take to the sea in fragile boats, hoping that God would guide them to a suitable island retreat, is satirised in Simon Young's book *A.D. 500*, published in 2005. Here Young imagines a party of sophisticated Greeks from the Byzantine empire visiting the British Isles at the beginning of the sixth century. The narrator of the book warns his readers that if they should ever visit Dalriada they should 'on no account travel to northern Britain in the boat of one of the monks of Iona', as 'most of these desert seekers are never heard of again'. Among the monks who were never heard of again, at least in Ireland, may have been the Papar, the Irish brothers who are supposed to have discovered Iceland, and sustained a community there until the Norsemen arrived to settle the island in 874 CE.

One advantage of Iona as a setting for a monastery was that there were smaller islands nearby that could be used by solitary monks, or brothers in small groups, who felt the need to retreat into deeper isolation. Aidan himself used the island of Inner Farne, to the east and a little to the south of Lindisfarne, as his own solitary retreat. This tiny island would later become a favourite hermitage for St Cuthbert who, with Oswald and Aidan, is remembered as a member of the triumvirate of great northern saints.

Aidan had been a monk on Iona, a rather bigger island than Lindisfarne, which is one of the scatter of Hebridean islands that lie off the craggy western 'face' of Scotland. Like Lindisfarne, Iona is unusually interesting from the geological point of view. Whereas Lindisfarne is made of volcanic rock, much of Iona rests on Lewisian gneiss, a very ancient kind of rock which, at over two thousand million years old, pre-dates life on Earth.

The monastery there had been founded in 563 by Columba, the monk who had been so useful to the Irish poets who had been trying to reconstruct the text of the epic *Tain*. Presumably many island monks sought out their lonely refuges to be closer to God and to pray and go about their holy business without too many interruptions or distractions, but according to one story Columba had an additional reason.

The monk who had supposedly helped to reconstruct *The Tain* had also made a copy of a book of psalms owned by St Finnian of Movilla. Unfortunately Columba had not asked

Finnian's permission to do this: he had worked secretly, at night, his work lit only by his miraculously-glowing fingers. A dispute over Columba's right to keep his copy escalated into a military conflict. Perhaps three thousand men died at the resulting Battle of Cúl Dreimhne in around 560, and the guilt-ridden Columba was advised to leave Ireland altogether and live in exile somewhere out of sight of the land of his fathers. He hoped to be able to use Iona as a base from which to spread the gospel to the Picts: the plan was to win as many converts to Christianity as there had been dead bodies after the Battle of Cúl Dreimhne. Columba's mission to the Northern Picts was unusual because he was in charge of it, although he was only an abbot, not a bishop like Aidan.

Columba's ability to provoke a war (if this really happened) and the widespread respect that was accorded him may be attributed to the fact that he was of aristocratic blood. His missionary efforts were not, however, welcomed by everyone. When he approached the castle of King Brude near Inverness the gates were closed and bolted against him. But when Columba made the sign of the cross, the bolts shot back and the gates flew open. After such a demonstration of holy power, King Brude was more than ready to listen to Columba's preaching, and soon agreed to be baptised.

The power of the Irish saint was also felt by a figure familiar to the readers of English tabloid newspapers, especially during the summer 'silly season' when the papers sometimes struggle to find decent stories. Arriving at Loch Ness, Columba and his party saw a man being buried on the shore, and learned that he had just been killed by the loch's famous monster. Undaunted, the saint ordered one of his group to swim across the lake to fetch a boat for them. When 'Nessie' started to chase the swimmer, Columba's power held him back.

Columba had died when Aidan was a small boy. While modern visitors to both Iona and Lindisfarne can see the remains of later stone buildings, the original monasteries built by Columba and Aidan would have been wooden structures, perhaps with wattle-and-daub walls and thatched roofs. Such buildings were horribly susceptible to fire, especially in those days when people depended on naked flames for both warmth and light. This was probably one reason why the Anglo-Saxons put up separate buildings to serve as chapels, kitchens, mead-halls, workshops and dormitories, while later generations would incorporate many of these as separate rooms within one large stone or brick structure, building chapels into castles, for instance.

There is little evidence about what Aidan's monastery on Lindisfarne looked like, but there is no reason to suppose that it was very different from his old home, Columba's foundation on Iona. This is supposed to have been enclosed in a protective *rath* or *vallum* – a rampart of earth or stones. Inside this were the church, the refectory, Columba's private hut, the huts belonging to the other monks, and a guest-house or *hospitium*. Outside the *rath* there would have been a shed for cows, barns, a smithy, a stable, a carpenter's workshop, a kiln and a water-mill. The monks would probably have worn rough, home-spun habits and shaved their heads in the style of the Celtic tonsure: completely bald at the front but with hair growing freely behind an imaginary vertical line stretching over the top of the head from ear to ear.

To the untrained eye, monasteries like Columba's original humble foundation on Iona would have been indistinguishable from many secular settlements, particularly in Ireland. In Aidan's day, Ireland was quite innocent of towns and cities, as parts of Northumbria still were much later in the Middle Ages. The Irish lived in tiny, scattered settlements, huts huddled inside their defensive *raths*. The pagan equivalents of Christian monasteries, occupied by druids and their followers, may also have followed the same pattern.

Since these modest monasteries were usually made of extremely perishable materials, there is little left of them to be uncovered by modern archaeologists. One exception is the island of Skellig Michael off the south-west coast of Ireland, where the lack of wood and thatch forced the monks to build in stone. The monastery here may have been a going concern in Aidan's day, and visitors can still see steep stone stairs, paths, terraces, walls, a graveyard, stone crosses and dry-stone, dome-shaped buildings left behind by the monks. All of this looks so striking that the island was used as a location for scenes in three recent Star Wars films.

It is hard to credit, but monasteries like the one on Iona, where many modern people would struggle to survive at all, became important centres of learning, and produced manuscripts of copied or original texts that have survived till today, and are treasured as some of the greatest masterpieces of world culture. Libraries were added to the monastery buildings, and also *scriptoria* – special buildings where texts could be copied. Research into Bede's writings has revealed that he had access to at least one hundred and fifty books – a prodigious number in those days before printing and cheap paper. This suggests that the monasteries of Wearmouth and Jarrow had impressive libraries for their time, since they may have possessed a number of books Bede never used, and perhaps duplicates of the ones he did use.

In this context 'access to' does not mean that Bede necessarily had all of his hundred and fifty plus books to hand. We know that he corresponded with a monk called Nothhelm, who was helping the chronicler by searching through the papal archives in Rome: Notthelm also researched the Christian history of Kent. Nothhelm, who died in 739, became Archbishop of Canterbury in 735. It is likely that it was Nothhelm who discovered the story, re-told by Bede, of Lucius, the second-century British king who wrote to Pope Eleutherius, asking for help with the business of converting his people to the Christian faith. Nothhelm may have found Lucius in a history of the popes that he consulted while he was in Rome, but some experts suspect that the Lucius he discovered lived in what is now Turkey and had nothing to do with Britain at all. Bede himself may never have seen many of the books and other documents that Notthelm consulted on his behalf: presumably the researcher sent him extracts or summaries.

Despite the fact that they were separate from each other, the individual buildings inside the ramparts at Bamburgh would have been little more fire-proof than those on Iona or Lindisfarne, a fact which was surely understood by Penda, the pagan king of Mercia, who continued to be an enemy of the Northumbrians after the death of King Oswald.

Some time near the end of Aidan's life, during the reign of Oswald's brother King Oswiu, Penda's Mercians raided Northumbria. As usual, Bede can only give us the briefest summary of what happened: it is tempting to extrapolate from this to paint a more detailed picture. It is likely that the occupants of the little village that lay in the shadow of the fortress of Bamburgh collected what valuables they had and fled into the fortress itself, as soon as news of Penda's approaching army reached them. It is unclear whether the Mercians advanced overland or raided by sea. If they did both, it is hard to see how the land and sea elements of the audacious raid could could have been coordinated, given the technology of the time.

It may be that things quickly became overcrowded inside Bamburgh's ramparts, especially if the occupants of Oswald's other seat, at Yeavering, also fled there, knowing that the seaside fortress would be better able to withstand a siege.

Did some or all of the Lindisfarne monks also flee to the fortress, or did they trust in God to protect them on their semi-island? They could hardly expect Penda's troops to spare them out of respect for their holiness: Penda's determination to give the Northumbrians a hard time may have been motivated in part by a dislike for their religion.

Bede tells us that during these events Aidan was at his solitary hermitage on the tiny island of Inner Farne. Were more of the Lindisfarne monks hiding away in scattered bolt-holes together with the monastery's most precious possessions; the holy manuscripts, the communion plate and the more elaborate ceremonial vestments? Given enough warning, some of the monks might even have planned a return to Iona, or somewhere else north of Northumbria itself.

It may be that, because the settlements near Bamburgh had had adequate warning of his approach, Penda and his troops found nothing but empty buildings around the fortress, and at the monastery on Lindisfarne itself. No worthwhile booty, and little or nothing to feed his soldiers, who were now a long way from home, and surely beyond the reach of any practicable supply-lines stretching from Penda's base in Mercia. Looking up at the huge wooden gates of the fortress, the pagan king probably realised that a conventional siege would take too long. His men might grow hungry, and try to stage a mutiny out of desperation.

Oswiu might also have been able to get a message to one of his other seats, or one or more of his allies, and as a result reinforcements might already be on the way, spoiling for a fight with Penda, and more than ready to raise any siege. Penda probably already knew about Bamburgh's internal water-supply, that could not be interrupted, or poisoned, from the outside, and may even have been given a rough estimate of how long the grain stored in the city's granaries would last.

The Mercian monarch decided to order the demolition of all the nearby villages which, Bede tells us, enabled him to bring to the base of Bamburgh's rock 'an immense quantity of beams, rafters, partitions, wattles and thatch, wherewith he encompassed the place to a great height on the land side, and when he found the wind favourable, he set fire to it and attempted to burn the town'. Penda's idea might have been to smoke out Oswiu and his followers or, if the fire actually spread on to the top of the rock, to force them out through the gates as the flames raged through the great hall, the church and the other buildings.

Penda's decision, to risk the total destruction of the fortress of Bamburgh, looks a bit desperate. One can imagine him screaming at his captains, 'We've got to do *something*; we've come *all this way*.' To attempt this, he had already destroyed some villages, so if he had managed to gain control of the Bamburgh fortress itself he might have found himself in charge of nothing more than a wilderness of ashes and post-holes. It may be that he did not plan to take control at all, but merely intended to unnerve King Oswiu, weaken his power and disrupt his kingdom.

With his base at Bamburgh compromised and needing reconstruction, Oswiu might have been less keen to try to reunite Northumbria and regain control of all the places his brother Oswald had once ruled over. If the people from the villages Penda had dismantled now needed to be sheltered in the fortress, a great deal of annoyance and frustration may have dogged King Oswiu's future attempts to assert his power and plan retaliation.

Presumably King Oswiu's lookouts began shooting arrows and javelins at Penda's men as soon as they approached the base of the rock, whether they were carrying firewood or flaming torches, or not. Something like the siege-scene shown on the lid of the Franks Casket might have unfolded, with the addition of heaps of kindling and, perhaps, the besieged throwing buckets of well-water down the sides of the rock. As the flames crept higher, Oswiu's people might have tried to dampen the outer walls of their box-rampart, to stop them bursting into flame.

Although Penda had set the fire on the landward side of the fortress, Bede tells us that Aidan was still able to see the conflagration from his vantage-point on Inner Farne, although in theory the fortress and its rock should have blocked his view. Bede writes that:

. . . he is said to have lifted up his eyes and hands to heaven, and cried with tears, "Behold, Lord, how great evil is wrought by Penda!" These words were hardly uttered, when the wind immediately veering from the city, drove back the flames upon those who had kindled them, so that some being hurt, and all afraid, they forebore any further attempts against the city, which they perceived to be protected by the hand of God.

Miracle or no miracle, it is eminently possible that the wind *did* change, making Penda's attempt at firing the fortress more hazardous for his own men than it became for Oswiu's people. It is also likely that, whatever the wind was doing, it soon became clear to Penda that the fire was never going to seriously inconvenience anyone in the fortress, and that, as they burned, the 'beams, rafters, partitions, wattles and thatch' were bound to fall or slide down the side of the rock and threaten to hurt the Mercian king and his followers.

Sometimes Bede tells us how a story reached him: in some cases, he had interviewed actual witnesses of events, or people who had themselves spoken to such witnesses. For Penda's fire at Bamburgh, which happened perhaps eighty years before he was writing, and over twenty before he was born, Bede does not give us any such authority, and resorts to the phrase 'he is said to have'.

If Aidan was alone on Inner Farne at the time, nobody could have seen him praying for the salvation of the fortress. Did he tell people later that he had prayed, or did locals who had seen or heard of the sudden change of wind-direction, so favourable to the Northumbrians, attribute it to Aidan's prayers, since they knew he had been nearby at the time?

V. Oswine, Oswiu and Penda

Penda's attempt to burn down Bamburgh, or perhaps smoke out its occupants, was one of a series of raids the Mercian king carried out against the Northumbrians after the death of Oswald. As far as we know, it was the raid that got closest to the heart of Oswald's northern kingdom of Bernicia.

For Bede, Penda, who may have been in his forties when he tried to smoke out Oswiu, was a stubborn, vindictive, deluded demon-worshipper. He inspired such terror in the East Anglians that when his attack was imminent they followed a completely irrational course of action. They forced their old king Sigeberht onto the battlefield, though he had given up his throne to become a monk, and refused to bear arms. As a result, Sigeberht met a martyr's end, standing unarmed on the field of battle, wearing only his monk's habit.

Modern readers, who may not share Bede's dread of paganism, might find it possible to think of Penda as just another petty Anglo-Saxon king who was busy doing what they all did. Seeing neighbouring kingdoms forming alliances, perhaps on the basis that they shared the new Christian religion, the pagan Penda sought to disrupt connections that might have threatened his own position. Some historians have suggested that Penda may have lived through periods when he lacked influence, and even a crown. His various wars might therefore have been in part attempts to regain lost power and prestige. Even Bede had to admit that Penda met with some success as a monarch, and the Anglo-Saxon Chronicle states that the Mercian ruled over his people for thirty years.

Although Bede says he was 'a most vigorous man', Penda evidently did not feel the need to make war against everybody all the time. Early in his reign he made a treaty with the West Saxons, and we know that he allied himself to Cadwallon of Gwynedd so that they could stand together against the Northumbrian king, Edwin. Later, Penda probably allied himself with the Welsh again, to defeat Oswald, perhaps at Oswestry: this time his ally may have been a king of Powys rather than Gwynedd.

By allying himself with at least two Welsh kings Penda showed that, though he personally was determined to remain a pagan, he was at least able to do business with Christians. He allowed Christian missionaries to proselytise in his own kingdom of Mercia, and even married his daughter Cyneburh to one of King Oswiu's sons. Later, he allowed his son Paeda to marry one of Oswiu's daughters. Unfortunately this alliance did not secure a lasting peace between the kings of Mercia and Northumbria: Penda was killed in battle against his Christian relative Oswiu in 655. As at Heavenfield, the Northumbrian force defeated a much larger army. On this occasion, Penda commanded 'thirty legions', including troops led by, among others, a king of the East Angles, and Oswald's son Ethelwald.

It is likely that Penda would not have dared to penetrate as deep into Northumbria as Bamburgh if his old enemy King Oswald had still been alive. With the death of Oswald in August

642, Northumbria broke up into its constituent parts of Bernicia in the north and Deira to the south, though Aidan continued to be bishop of both sub-kingdoms. As we have seen, the battle where Penda and his allies killed Oswald may have happened at Oswestry in Shropshire, on the border between Mercia and Powys. It is believed that a skull that rests in St Cuthbert's tomb under the flagstones of Durham Cathedral may be Oswald's. When the skull was examined at the end of the nineteenth century, it was found that the way the bones had been broken was consistent with the damage having been done at the time of death. A Doctor Selby Plummer guessed that the Saxon king had been felled by a blow to one side of his head then, as he lay sprawling on the ground, he was finished off with a heavier blow to the other side.

Penda ordered that Oswald's head and arms be displayed on stakes at the site of the battle. As we know, one legend states that a raven transferred the dead king's arm to a nearby tree. This may be why Oswestry has the name it has – 'Oswald's Tree'. When Oswald's head and arms had been exposed in this way, perhaps as a grisly offering to Woden, for about a year, his brother Oswiu collected them and took them back to his kingdom of Bernicia.

If Oswald's body-parts had indeed been displayed near Oswestry, his brother Oswiu's trip to collect them was a considerable journey of well over two hundred miles, some of it across enemy territory. The Bernician king presumably had to take a small army with him, all of whom would have needed to be fed and watered, as would their horses. Oswiu may have felt that the effort was worthwhile, not just because he wanted to show respect for his dead brother and give him a Christian burial, but also because the journey itself (which had some of the features of a pious pilgrimage) and the re-capture of the remains might confer both prestige and legitimacy on himself, the new lord of Bamburgh. The boldness of the plan might also have boosted Oswiu's reputation, although he was not actually taking the much riskier step of going to war. The fact that, after the trip, he brought some of Oswald's remains back to Bernicia meant, of course, that nobody else could claim to have them. If God was thought to have smiled on Oswiu's project, that might look like the Almighty conferring his blessing on Oswiu's monarchy. Bede does not tell us whether Aidan had anything to do with Oswiu's expedition: would the bishop have approved?

Bede gives a lengthy account of the miracles associated with Oswald's remains, and even with the site where his death occurred. A sick horse, and a young girl who was suffering from a form of paralysis, were healed just by visiting the site of the pious king's martyrdom, and even dirt from the site was believed to have healing powers. So many pilgrims took away samples of this miraculous soil that they eventually made a hole as deep as a man is tall.

A linen bag of Oswald's miraculous dirt was taken away by a traveller who then stopped at an inn. He hung his bag up on a post, and when the whole building was burned down later that night, it was found that the bag and the post had not been touched by the fire.

Many years after Oswald's death in battle, when a plague was sweeping through Britain and Ireland, a Scottish scholar felt himself coming down with the symptoms of the pestilence, but was cured by drinking water into which a fragment of the oak stake on which Oswald's head had been displayed had been dipped. This may have been the plague that hit the British Isles in 664, which was one of the many waves of plague that spread throughout Europe and beyond between 541 and 767. It is interesting that the stake, just one splinter of which was thought to have miraculous properties, was made of oak. Oaks were associated with both the Norse god Thor and the Roman god Jupiter.

Perhaps because Oswald's body had already been dismembered by Penda or his followers, Oswiu and his family seemed to think that it might be a good idea to take advantage of this and bury bits of him in different places. While the pious king's head was buried at Lindisfarne, and his miraculously-preserved arm was encased in a silver shrine at Bamburgh, other parts were taken by Oswiu's sister Osthryth to Bardney Abbey in Lincolnshire. The monks there were reluctant to take the relics at first: Bardney was not in Northumbria, but in the rival kingdom of Lindsey, south of the Humber. Oswald's bones were left in a tent outside the abbey all night; where they were illuminated by a bright pillar of light through all the hours of darkness. This convinced the monks to accept the bones.

Penda's repeated attacks, such as the one on Bamburgh itself, had caused Oswiu to lose control of Deira, and probably of many other places that Oswald had either ruled or had influence over. The Bernician king was also troubled by his scheming nephews, Alchfrid and Oidilwald. Bede claimed that Oswald had 'brought under his dominion all the nations and provinces of Britain, which are divided into four languages, to wit, those of the Britons, the Picts, the Scots, and the English'. After Oswald's death, his brother Oswiu ruled in Bernicia, while their nephew Oswine took control of Deira.

Oswine was a son of Osric, the king of Deira who had been killed by Penda's ally Cadwallon in 633 or 634. As we know, Osric had been besieging the king of Gwynedd, who was holed up in a walled city, perhaps York; but Cadwallon sallied out with a large force and demolished Osric's army. Although, like Oswald, Osric had become a Christian during the brothers' exile among the Celts, he reverted to paganism when he became king of Deira. This had no doubt been a big disappointment to many of the Deirans who had been baptised under King Edwin.

Although his father had been an 'apostate' or traitor to the faith, Bede depicts his son Oswine as an exemplary Christian king. He was tall, good-looking, friendly and generous, and inspired love and loyalty from his subjects.

Bede gives a touching instance of Oswine's humility. One day, the young king took it into his head to give a very fine horse to Bishop Aidan as a gift. This would have been in keeping with the gift-giving tradition of the Saxon kings, and no doubt the lord of Deira thought that a worthy mount might help Aidan in his task of tirelessly visiting every corner of his diocese. Aidan accepted the horse, but when he saw a beggar on the road he dismounted and immediately gave the poor man his magnificent new beast 'with all its royal trappings'.

Oswine was furious when he heard about this. 'Why did you give that poor man your royal horse,' he demanded of Aidan, 'when we have plenty of horses of less value, and lots of other things, that you could have given him? I personally had chosen that horse, and set it aside for you!' When he said this, Oswine had just come in from a day's hunting, and was getting ready to eat dinner with his bishop.

'Your majesty, what do you mean?' asked Aidan. 'Is the son of a mare more dear to you than the son of God?' After an awkward few minutes, that passed while Oswine was silently warming himself by the fire, the king took off his sword and kneeled at Aidan's feet, begging his forgiveness. The bishop was moved to tears, and forgave the king.

They sat down to dinner, but Aidan continued to weep. One of his priests asked him, in Irish (which Oswine did not understand) what was wrong. 'I prophesy that this king cannot live long,' Aidan replied. 'I never saw a humble monarch before, and he will soon be snatched away, because his nation does not deserve such a ruler'.

The story as presented by Bede rings true, and there are no miraculous elements in it, extraordinary as Aidan's gesture of giving away his horse might seem. True, Aidan's prophesy could be interpreted as a miraculous inspiration from God, but it can also be read as a moment of simple insight, such as many people are granted. The details of the post-hunting, pre-dinner scene are also entirely convincing, and the fact that the bishop is still sad after his reconciliation with the king adds a touch of the unexpected that also seems very real.

Oswine should not have been surprised that Aidan was not frightened to offend him by passing on his princely present. Bede tells us that the bishop could be very outspoken in his criticism of the behaviour of the rich and powerful, so the experience of annoying some magnate would not have been new to him. Though Aidan was happy to give away anything that he owned to beggars, 'he never gave money to the powerful men of the world, but only food, if he happened to entertain them'.

When he was not giving money or other donations to the poor, the bishop used his wealth 'in ransoming such as had been wrongfully sold for slaves', a reminder that slavery was still a fact of life in Anglo-Saxon England. Bede adds that Aidan 'made many of those he had ransomed his disciples, and after having taught and instructed them, advanced them to priest's orders'.

It is likely that Aidan did not give away his gift-horse just because he wanted to help a beggar. He always made a point of travelling around his diocese on foot, something that would literally have put him on the same level as the common people. A horse, especially an impressive royal horse, would have given him a physical dominance that, together with his use of English as a second language, may have made it harder for him to communicate effectively. Aidan might also have been remembering the example of Jesus, who either walked everywhere or rode on a donkey or a colt (see Matthew 21:6-7).

Bede tells us that Aidan's habit of travelling everywhere on foot, when practicable, allowed him to:

. . . turn aside to any whomsoever he saw, whether rich or poor, and call upon them, if infidels, to receive the mystery of the faith, or, if they were believers, strengthen them in the faith, and stir them up by words and actions to giving of alms and the performance of good works.

Aidan's gift-horse is referred to as male, as the 'son of a mare'. If he had been a mettlesome stallion, bred to carry a king to battle, Aidan might also have been concerned that the control and management of such an animal might present problems in a monastic stable.

Like the story of Oswald's gift of the silver plate, and the narrative encapsulated in the Christmas song *Good King Wenceslaus*, the tale of Aidan's gift-horse leaves us wanting more. What on earth happened to the beggar who suddenly acquired such a magnificent horse? Did he attempt to sell it?

Did he get into trouble because people thought that he must have stolen it? We can imagine a historical novel where the man turns out to be a nobleman who has lost his land and fallen on hard times. On his magnificent new beast, he rides back to the ruins of his old fortress and retrieves his weapons and armour, carefully buried under a wall. Thus equipped, and newly washed and barbered, he joins the army of some local king and lives again as an honoured thegn, boozing and feasting in the mead-hall.

An excellent essay by Jennifer Neville of Royal Holloway College, London sheds light on the story of Oswine, Aidan and the gift-horse (for details, see bibliography). Neville's main purpose in her essay *Stalking a Dark Horse* was to look closely at the horses mentioned in the Anglo-Saxon epic *Beowulf*, but she mentions the story of Oswine, Aidan and the magnificent gift-horse, and her findings are relevant to the tale Bede tells.

Neville implies that the chronicler's use of the term 'royal horse' (*equus regius*) may have been an attempt to render into Latin one of a number of terms used in the Old English or Anglo-Saxon language for a horse fit for a noble or a king: 'friþhengest', 'steda', 'blanca', 'mearh' or 'wicg'. A horse bred specifically for war was an 'eoh', and the intriguing term 'wintersteal' was also applied to very good horses. The word may denote a beast kept in a stall and fed throughout the winter, at great expense.

In Neville's essay we are reminded not only that there were many wild or forest horses living in Aidan's Britain, but that such horses, left to fend for themselves throughout the year, tend to evolve into small, hardy ponies unsuitable for riding, especially by grown men in armour, carrying spears, swords and shields. Such horses, captured and fenced in by humans, can produce larger, stronger offspring after several generations, as long as they are well-fed, and their breeding is controlled. These horses are 'set aside', like Aidan's horse had been by King Oswine himself, and are valuable not only because of the trouble and expense of their care, but also because they can be used to breed even more large, strong specimens. Further improvements to such blood-lines could be effected by bringing in superior stud-animals from abroad.

Britain still has wild or forest horses, and modern conservationists believe that they may have an important role to play in the 're-wilding' of our landscape, which may be necessary to avoid environmental disaster. New Forest and Exmoor ponies are examples of these kinds of equines.

If Aidan's horse had been 'set aside' for deluxe treatment, the 'horses of less value' that King Oswine mentions may have been 'unimproved' horses; tame or domesticated examples of the small wild or forest equines, suitable only to carry packs, or to pull small carts. Something between one of these diminutive, dun-coloured animals and the magnificent steed that Oswine gave Aidan might have been a more suitable gift for the bishop, whom Bede tells us would sometimes ride a horse if he needed to get somewhere in a hurry.

Jennifer Neville also mentions an early eleventh-century Anglo-Saxon bishop, of Winchester, who accepted the windfall of a fine black stallion via the will of a royal prince, though he probably already possessed a number of impressive equines, and may even have owned one or more stud-farms. Evidently, Aidan did not want to become such an opulent prince of the church.

Aidan's prophecy about the early death of Oswine turned out to be all too prescient. Perhaps because his continued rule as king of Deira was an obstacle to Oswiu's ambition of reuniting the whole of Northumbria under his own control, the king of Bernicia marched on his nephew's kingdom with a large army. When Oswine realised just how big Oswiu's force really was, he disbanded his own troops and, accompanied only by a faithful thegn called Tondhere, sought sanctuary with his friend Hunwald, probably at Gilling in North Yorkshire. But Hunwald betrayed his guests, and an assassin called Ethilwin killed both Oswine and Tondhere.

By putting away his nephew Oswine, Oswiu had also killed his second wife's second cousin. This lady was Eanfled, a daughter of King Edwin. She had fled to Kent after the death of her father, but of course needed to be brought back north to marry Oswiu, the king of Bernicia. In 642, nine years before Oswine was killed, a priest called Utta was detailed to fetch her, but it seems he was a little nervous about the responsibility. Before he set off, he went to visit Aidan, to beg him to pray for a safe journey for himself and the princess. The bishop gave him a phial of holy oil, prophesying as he did so that, during their return by sea, Utta and Eanfled would encounter some rough weather. 'Cast this oil on the water,' Aidan suggested, 'and the wind will cease immediately: then you will have nothing but fair weather for the rest of your voyage'.

Like Aidan's later prophecy about the death of Oswine, this prediction turned out to be accurate; and the oil poured on the troubled waters did indeed calm them. Unfortunately, the stress of the storm caused Utta to forget both the oil and Aidan's prophecy, until the ship had taken on so much water that everybody on board thought that they were about to drown. At last something jogged the priest's memory, and he stilled the storm with his phial of oil. Bede tells us that he heard this story from one Cynimund, 'a most faithful priest', who had heard it from Utta himself. One can imagine Oswiu's new bride arriving, still shivering a little with fright, in her battered ship, at the base of the rock on which the Bamburgh fortress stood, in those days when the waves still broke against the rock itself.

To try to atone for the murder of his relative, Oswiu ordered that a new monastery be built at Gilling, the site of the assassination. It may be that Aidan's reaction to the death of Oswine was one of the factors that made Oswiu feel that he needed to atone. The good bishop could hardly have taken the news harder. He died just twelve days after Oswine, in the village that lay in the shadow of the Bamburgh fortress, which by this time, it would seem, had been at least partially re-built after Penda had reduced it to kindling.

When the bishop was taken ill, they propped him up against a wooden buttress on the outside of the local church. Thinking, perhaps, that he should not be moved, they set up a tent around him, to shelter him. After he died, propped up in this position, he was buried in the monks' churchyard on Lindisfarne, though his remains were later translated to a new church on the island.

But Penda was not yet finished with the little village. He burned it again, though this time without stacking it up against the rock below the nearby fortress. As the smoke cleared it was found that, though the rest of the church had burned down, Aidan's buttress was unscorched, just like the post at the inn where the traveller had hung his bag of Oswald's holy dirt.

The ruined church was re-built in the same place, but was burned down again, this time by accident. Again the buttress remained whole, though the heat of the second fire had been so intense that the iron nails that had been driven into the wooden support had melted away. When the church was re-built again, the buttress was placed inside as a holy relic. After that, healing miracles were associated with it, and people experienced miraculous cures after drinking water with splinters of the buttress immersed in it.

The story of Aidan's death, propped up on a buttress and, oddly, not lying flat, may have had an influence on the sculptor Kathleen Parbury, who created a red concrete sculpture of the saint in 1958. The statue can be seen in St Mary's churchyard on Aidan's island of Lindisfarne, and images of it are regularly seen on the covers of books about the Northern Saints. Here we see Aidan, clean-shaven, gaunt and sombre in his monk's habit, standing, but also apparently propped up, not on a buttress, but against a Celtic-style cross. His resigned, other-worldly expression may indeed have been Aidan's expression as he lay dying, or, rather, as he died in a seated position. Parbury's Aidan carries a plain bishop's crook in one hand and, as in many depictions of the saint, a flaming torch in the other.

VI. Aidan's Legacy

Although Bede devotes very few pages in his *Ecclesiastical History* to Aidan, a truly pivotal figure, he still seems to have felt he had space to raise a particular objection to the bishop's approach – twice. The chronicler's issue concerned the system Aidan and his fellow Celtic Christians used to calculate the correct date for Easter.

Whereas in the Western tradition Christmas, a very well-behaved festival in this respect, takes place on the twenty-fifth of December every year, Easter Sunday is sometimes as early as March the twenty-second, and as late as April the twenty-fifth. This can cause all sorts of problems, especially for organisations like schools and colleges whose terms follow the traditional pattern of the Christian year. And when Easter Sunday moves, the build-up to Easter has to move as well, so that in 2021 Lent began on the seventeenth of February, but in 2020 it started nine days later; and in 2019 it began on the sixth of March.

These days people know when Easter is going to happen because of calendars and diaries, and their electronic equivalents. If they have developed the bad habit of not looking at their diaries or calendars often enough, they might get a hint that Easter is coming when Easter cards and eggs begin to appear in the shops. They might also catch some reference to the upcoming festival on the TV or radio, or among social media posts.

The situation was quite different for the Christians of Aidan's time, some of whom had little or no regular contact with people outside their local area. The monks who had sought God in isolated places like Iona and Skellig Michael needed some way to calculate the date of Easter for themselves. To do this, they also needed to keep an accurate calendar all through the year, in those days before people could just buy a new one every year from a shop.

Bede mentions that the Celtic Christians of Aidan's time claimed that they were following a widely-approved system developed by Anatolius, a third-century bishop of Laodicea, an ancient city in what is now Syria. Anatolius favoured a system whereby, to put it very simply, the same nineteen-year calendar was repeated, every nineteen years.

Everybody knows that to use the same one-year calendar or diary for more than one year would be foolish. I am writing this chapter on the fifteenth of January 2022, which is a Saturday. Last year, 2021, the same date was a Friday, and in 2020 it was a Wednesday. If I was continuing to follow my 2020 calendar throughout 2021 and the beginning of 2022, I would be 'lost in time' like some hero of science fiction, forever thinking it was the wrong day. Clearly, to repeat the same *annual* calendar is not a good idea, but Anatolius and his supporters believed that his nineteen-year calendar could be repeated without the users losing track of where they were in a given year or, very importantly, celebrating Easter on the wrong day.

Bede, who even wrote a book called *On the Reckoning of Time*, favoured the nineteen-year rotation partly because he knew of a system whereby people could count to nineteen on the fingers of one hand. The chronicler did not approve an alternative system, used by the Celtic Christians, that employed an eighty-four year cycle. What we might call the '84 system', where an eighty-four year calendar is repeated, had been a bone of contention between St Augustine of Canterbury and the British Christians over a century before Bede wrote his history. At an ill-tempered meeting around 603 CE Augustine begged the British to adopt the Roman approach, in this and other matters, but they would not comply.

The exact nature of the 84 system was rather mysterious until 1985, when the Irish historian Dáibhí Ó Cróinín discovered a table, called a *latercus*, setting out the details, in a library in Padua. Analysis of the table suggested that it must have been copied, by a tenth-century Celtic Christian, from one first set down in 438 CE, over one hundred and fifty years before Augustine of Canterbury landed in Kent.

The analysts also discovered that the 84 system as represented in the table came up with Easter Sundays between the twenty-sixth of March and the twenty-third of April, a rather narrower range of possible dates than we find in the modern Western system. A document kept in Munich has also revealed that none of the months in the Celtic Christian calendar had twenty-eight or thirty-one days. They were all either twenty-nine or thirty days in length. For the Celts, February always had twenty-nine days, whereas in the modern West it only reaches that number in a leap-year. Because the Celts were really using the 84 system, their claim that they were following Anatolius of Laodicea was viewed with suspicion by the Roman Christians.

Whatever the virtues of the 84 system, and its similarities to the nineteen-year cycle of Anatolius, it had been discredited by the Roman Christians, and by the early 630s many of the Celtic Christians of southern Ireland had abandoned it. But in the north the Irish continued to stick to it, as did the monks of Iona and Lindisfarne, including Aidan himself. Bede implies that the Northumbrians who looked to Aidan as their bishop supported the outdated system out of respect for him, and that some of this respect rubbed off on Finan, Aidan's successor. By the time of Finan's own successor Colman, however, many felt that a change was overdue. Colman should not, of course, be confused with Corman, Aidan's unsuccessful predecessor as missionary to Northumbria.

We have already met Eanfled, King Oswiu's second wife, who was raised in Kent, learned the Roman form of Christianity and had been escorted to Northumbria by Utta. Utta it was who had stilled a dangerous storm at the last moment by deploying Aidan's miraculous oil, and thus safely brought Eanfled to King Oswiu. Eanfled was in the habit of celebrating Easter on the Roman date, while Oswiu, who had been baptised into the Celtic way, used the Celtic date. During some Easters, therefore, the king and queen celebrated Easter on different Sundays, so that while one of them was feasting, the other was fasting.

A version of this situation will be familiar to many modern people who live in truly international cities, such as London, New York and Paris. In 2021, for instance, Anglicans and Roman Catholics celebrated Easter Sunday on the fourth of April; while the Greek, Russian and Ethiopian Orthodox Christians celebrated it on the second of May. Although attempts have been made over the years to reconcile the Western and Eastern systems, this disparity continues to cause confusion and inconvenience, or, to look on the bright side, adds diversity to the calendar and allows some people to enjoy two Easters.

King Oswiu, evidently tired of celebrating one Easter and merely watching another, during some years, arranged a synod to thrash out the issues. In this he may have been influenced by his son Alchfrid, who favoured the Roman way. The synod took place at Whitby in 664, where it was presided over by St Hilda, who had known Aidan well and was then abbess of Whitby.

The main action of the synod took place during a public debate between Colman, and Wilfrid, later made a saint, who represented the Roman point of view. Of all the celebrated Northern Saints, Wilfrid is perhaps the least attractive. His speeches at Whitby betray a showy and intolerant spirit. One feels that Aidan would never have spoken like this on such an occasion.

'The Easter which we keep,' Wilfrid argued, was observed in Rome, and also throughout 'Italy and in Gaul' and 'in Africa, Asia, Egypt, Greece, and all the world'. 'Only these,' he went on, perhaps pointing contemptuously at Colman and his supporters, 'and their accomplices in obstinacy, I mean the Picts and the Britons . . . strive to oppose all the rest of the world'. Wilfrid went on to demolish (as he no doubt saw it) Colman's argument that he was following the precepts of John the Apostle, and tried to show that the Celts were not, in fact, following Anatolius's formula, though Colman asserted that they had been doing so for years.

'What have you to do with him?' asked Wilfrid, meaning Anatolius, 'since you do not observe his decrees?' Wilfrid then went on to show that the Celts either did not know about, or despised, Anatolius's 'cycle of nineteen years'. Warming to his theme, Wilfrid addressed Colman's assertion that his Celtic forbears, including Columba, had not observed the Roman Easter, but were manifestly great saints. Here Wilfrid came close to suggesting that those old Celtic saints might be excluded from heaven because of their faulty calendar. 'When many, in the day of judgement,' he asserted 'shall say to our Lord, that in His name they have prophesied, and have cast out devils, and done many wonderful works, our Lord will reply, that He never knew them'.

Sensing, perhaps, that he might have gone too far, Wilfrid backed off a little and conceded that the old Celtic saints' observance of Easter probably did them no harm, since they proceeded 'with rude simplicity' and knew no better. But 'I believe,' Wilfrid added, 'that, if any teacher, reckoning after the Catholic manner, had come among them, they would have as readily followed his admonitions, as they are known to have kept those commandments of God, which they had learned and knew'.

Though some must have found it unduly aggressive, Wilfrid's rhetoric at the Synod of Whitby convinced King Oswiu, who decided against Columba and Colman, and in favour of Wilfrid, Rome, the Pope and St Peter. His kingdom now switched to the Roman Easter, and Colman and his followers returned to the land of the Scots. Colman was replaced as Bishop of Lindisfarne by Tuda.

As at Augustine's troubled meeting with the British Christians early in the seventh century, matters other than the correct date of Easter were discussed at Whitby, but Bede puts the so-called Paschal question very much in the foreground of his account. It was clearly regarded, at least by Bede, as a matter of great significance – note how the chronicler tells us that Wilfrid equated the correct keeping of Easter, as he saw it, with 'the commandments of God', and was even prepared to entertain the idea that Celtic saints such as Columba might be excluded from heaven because of their approach to Christianity's spring festival.

It is surely significant that although Wilfrid implied that Columba was wrong-headed, or at least rude and simple, in his approach to Easter, he did not mention Aidan, though if he had done so he would have had to assert that he was just as wrong as Columba. Maybe even Wilfrid was sensitive enough to realise that a negative criticism of that particular saint at Whitby might have given offence and perhaps even compromised the reception of his, Wilfrid's, case. Aidan had, after all, only been dead for thirteen years, and many of those present at the synod would have known and loved him. Having died over fifty years earlier, Columba was a more remote figure, associated not just with a more distant time, but with places other than Northumbria.

Although the Roman side could count the decision made at the Synod of Whitby as a victory, and although one suspects that Wilfrid felt triumphant, it is likely that some on both sides had a bad taste in their mouths when the meeting broke up. The fact that there were opposing sides at all was surely regrettable, as was the way that Columba's name and reputation had been called into question. More seriously, perhaps, Wilfrid had even cast shade on John the Apostle, the 'beloved disciple' of the Gospels. When Colman claimed that his church followed the Easter as marked by John, Wilfrid not only said that they didn't, but also that nobody should, since John was a Jew and to follow John's approach would be too Jewish. And so even at Whitby in

664, anti-Semitism, one of the nastiest Christian traits, just had to raise its head.

In theory, Wilfrid's performance at Whitby should have won him great advancement in his career, but the high-handed attitude that had characterised his rhetoric at the Synod complicated his next step up the ladder of ecclesiastical advancement. Consenting to be elected Bishop of Northumbria, he decided that no bishop in the British Isles was qualified to induct him into the episcopacy. He therefore proceeded to France, where he enjoyed an investiture according to his taste, during which he was carried around on a gold throne.

The gold throne was in keeping with Wifrid's personal style. He was derived from aristocratic parents, and he liked to be accompanied by a large and splendid retinue, and no doubt thought nothing of owning and riding splendid, highly-bred horses like the one Aidan had given away to a beggar. As well as a talent for pomp and circumstance, the new bishop had a tendency to rub people up the wrong way, and the rest of his career was characterised by disagreements, exile and even imprisonment. His biographer Stephen of Ripon claimed that he was humble, but many of Wilfrid's troubles must have stemmed from a form of vanity similar to that of Corman, Aidan's unsuccessful predecessor as missionary to the Northumbrians. In other words, like Corman, Wilfrid was everything Aidan had never been.

Some modern enthusiasts for Celtic Christianity regard the decision made by King Oswiu at the Synod of Whitby as an absolute disaster. Northumbria was not only turning its back on the Celtic Easter, it was rejecting Celtic Christianity in general, a form of the faith which some assume was more tolerant, less dictatorial and more in tune with nature than the Protestant and

Roman Catholic varieties. The idea that the Celts ran their own local form of Christianity without constant reference to Rome elicits a kind of nostalgic patriotism from people who seek out Celtic-themed prayer-books and other Celtic-inspired spiritual works.

The Northumbrian Christians did not, however, abandon the way of Aidan when they turned aside from the Celtic way. When Aidan died, a young man called Cuthbert saw angels coming down from heaven and gathering up the saint's radiant soul. Cuthbert was in a field at the time, guarding some sheep, but it seems that he was not a shepherd. When he turned up at the monastery of Melrose to offer himself as a novice, he arrived on a horse and carrying a spear, both signs of high social status among the Anglo-Saxons.

Cuthbert went on to become Bishop of Lindisfarne, as Aidan had been; but he belonged to the generation of Northumbrian believers who accepted the decision of the Synod of Whitby and embraced the Roman way (Cuthbert would have been around thirty years of age at the time of the Synod). His new Roman allegiance did not, however, prevent him from resembling Aidan in many respects, and we might say that the story of Saint Cuthbert is proof that the Celtic spirit did not leave Northumbria when Colman returned to the Scots.

Like Aidan, Cuthbert sought out remote islands on which to live as a hermit, and like his predecessor he liked to go on long walking-tours around his diocese, spreading the Word and encouraging the spiritually discouraged. Bede tells us that, like Aidan, Cuthbert seldom used a horse, which would literally have set him above the locals to whom he wanted to talk.

Some of Cuthbert's miracles, as related by Bede in his Life of the saint, resembled Aidan's (rather less numerous) miracles.

While Aidan's prayers changed the wind-direction at Bamburgh, thus preventing a disastrous fire, Cuthbert prayed that the wind would change to save the lives of some monks stranded on a raft in a fast-flowing river. This miracle-story, related near the start of Bede's *Life of Cuthbert*, is of great interest because while Cuthbert was praying for the monks, the peasants who stood with him on the bank were jeering at them and hoping that they would drown. They had introduced an incomprehensible new religion that had replaced the old ways, and now nobody knew what to do, they claimed. It was no doubt people of this sort whom Aidan and Cuthbert were most keen to meet and convert, on their long walks around their dioceses.

As well as his wind-and-water miracle, Cuthbert showed that the power of his prayers could utilise wind as a weapon to fight fire, as Aidan's had done. One piece of evidence that supports the idea that Cuthbert may have had an aristocratic background was that he had had a foster-mother, in his case a lady called Kenswyth. It seems that aristocratic families would often farm out the raising of their children to strangers. Kenswyth was a very virtuous woman, who later became a nun, and Cuthbert loved her and called her 'mother'.

During one of Cuthbert's frequent visits to his old foster-mother, who was by now a widow, the eastern edge of the village where she lived began to burn. The wind urged the fire on from house to house until it threatened Kenswyth's own home, but Cuthbert lay down on the ground and prayed, and the wind-direction changed, putting the house out of danger.

While Aidan had stilled a storm by a gift of holy oil, Cuthbert's prayers lifted a storm that kept him and his ship-mates stranded on a bleak part of the Scottish coast. The saint's faith also meant that the group, which was in danger of starving, found some fresh dolphin-meat on the beach. Cuthbert also used holy oil, in his case not to still a storm, but to cure an ailing young nun.

Bede tells us that two of Cuthbert's fire-taming miracles resembled similar miracles performed by two continental saints, but, in his *Life of Cuthbert*, the chronicler does not mention how Aidan's prayers saved the fortress of Bamburgh. It may be that the similarities between the lives and miracles of Aidan and Cuthbert are evident merely because they were both members of a long fellowship of Christian saints that stretched back to the New Testament. And many have compared the lives of saints from the New Testament and later to the lives of the Old Testament prophets.

It is tempting to compare Aidan's own career to the life of Samuel, as set out in the Old Testament (we have already seen how Bede compared King Oswald's father Ethelfrith to Samuel's older contemporary, King Saul). If, like many, Aidan had become a novice as a child, he resembled Samuel in this respect, since Samuel worked as a priest from an early age. The prophet's mother Hannah had promised that, if only the almighty would make her fertile, she would give her first son to God. Aidan might also have been promised to God by his pious parents back in Ireland. We might also compare Samuel's master, the priest Eli, to the abbots Aidan served under on Iona.

When he was a respected and experienced priest, Samuel picked out the tall, impressive-looking Saul as a the Hebrews' first king. According to the twelfth-century chronicler Reginald of Durham, Oswald was also tall and strong. Although Oswald was a king before Aidan came to Northumbria, so that there was no question of the new bishop picking him out, Aidan's acceptance of Oswald, implied in his cooperation with the Northumbrian monarch, must have added to his legitimacy, especially among the Christians of the neighbouring kingdom of Dalriada to the north.

At times, Samuel is very outspoken in his criticism of Saul, especially when Saul strays into Samuel's area of competence. Aidan could also speak truth to power, though there is no hint in Bede that the bishop ever threatened Oswald with God's disapproval. Samuel also kills Agag, an enemy king whom Saul has captured, who is brought to the prophet like a lamb to the slaughter. Samuel hacks Agag to pieces: it is hard to imagine the mild-mannered Aidan doing such a thing, though he too lived in violent and desperate times (1 Samuel 15:33).

Like Saul, Oswald's military and leadership skills expanded his sphere of influence, and sapped the power of his enemies, but during their reigns both Saul and Oswald were threatened by one particularly powerful enemy – in Saul's case the Philistines, and in Oswald's case, Penda, his Mercians and their allies. Both the Philistines and Penda followed religions that were in opposition to those of their enemies.

The Hebrews for whom Samuel was supposed to be the chief spiritual authority (including King Saul himself) had a tendency to backslide into sloppy observance of God's laws, and sometimes into outright idolatry. Bede makes it clear that Aidan was concerned to bring as many as he could to Christ, and to reinforce the faith of converts whose grasp on Christianity might be weakening.

Samuel transfers his loyalty from Saul to the future King David, when it becomes clear that God has deserted Saul. When Oswald was killed, Aidan transferred his loyalty to Oswine, the new king of Deira. Like Oswald, David was one of several brothers, and was not the eldest. We might compare Oswald's unlikely defeat of a larger army at Heavenfield to the famous passage where David, still a youngster, kills the giant Philistine champion, Goliath of Gath (1 Samuel 17).

The first book of Samuel gives us a lot of detail about David's encounter with Goliath. We learn exactly how tall the man from Gath was, what he wore, and the words of his challenge to the nervous Hebrew troops. We are also given details about where David got the fateful stone he used to kill Goliath, and how it lodged in the giant's forehead. We even learn about an attempt to put armour on David, which he takes off, preferring to meet Goliath unarmed, much as Beowulf fought the monster Grendel without arms or armour. Bede and his fellow monkish chroniclers tend not to go into that much detail about what happened during battles, perhaps because, as monks, they had no direct experience of such things.

When David marries Saul's daughter Michal, the conflict between the men takes on something of the character of a family row. Since Saul is trying to take David's life by some means, the prophet Samuel's friendship with David becomes a subversive relationship, where Samuel sometimes finds himself harbouring a fugitive. Aidan also found himself on the side of a fugitive leader, when Oswine went on the run from Oswiu. The conflict which eventually led to Oswine's murder was another family argument, since Oswiu was Oswine's uncle.

It may seem fanciful to compare a Christian bishop to an Old Testament prophet, but Bede himself does just this in his *Letter to Ecgbert*, written to bishop Ecgbert of York in 734. In his highly critical letter, Bede implies that the bishops of his own time were, in effect, stealing money from the people and not giving them anything back in return. By contrast, Bede reminds us, Samuel was able to ask the Hebrews 'whose ox have I taken? or whose ass have I taken? or whom have I defrauded? whom have I oppressed? or of whose hand have I received any bribe to blind mine eyes therewith?' (1 Samuel 12:3).

Aidan could no doubt have asked similar questions of the people of Northumbria, without anyone piping up to say that, yes, the saint had stolen from them or oppressed them. So far was Aidan from stealing someone's ass that, as we know, he gave away a magnificent horse that had been given to him by the ill-fated King Oswine. The saint's life is such an example of Christian virtue, humility and hard-working usefulness that even Bede, with his obsession with the correct calculation of Easter, was reluctant to condemn Aidan. Wrapping up his account of the saint, the chronicler reminded his readers that, though Aidan kept Easter on the wrong day:

in the celebration of his Easter, the object which he had at heart and reverenced and preached was the same as ours, to wit, the redemption of mankind, through the Passion, Resurrection and Ascension into Heaven of the Man Christ Jesus, who is the mediator between God and man.

Bede also reminds us that, though he sometimes kept the wrong Easter Sunday, Aidan did not fall into the terrible error of celebrating Easter on a day other than a Sunday, just because that day was 'on the fourteenth of the moon'.

At last, Bede found that he could put aside the whole Easter issue and list the things he admired about Aidan:

his love of peace and charity; of continence and humility; his mind superior to anger and avarice, and despising pride and vainglory; his industry in keeping and teaching the Divine commandments, his power of study and keeping vigil; his priestly authority in reproving the haughty and powerful, and at the same time his tenderness in comforting the afflicted, and relieving or defending the poor.

Select Bibliography

Adamnan (trans. William Reeves): *Life of Saint Columba*, Edmonston and Douglas, 1874

Alexander, Michael (trans.): *Beowulf*, Penguin, 2003

Bede (trans. J.A. Giles): *The Historical Works of the Venerable Bede*, Volume 2 , Bohn, 1843

Bede (trans. McLure, J. and Collins, R.: *The Ecclesiastical History of the English People*, Oxford, 1999

Boece, Hector (trans. John Bellenden): *The History and Chronicles of Scotland*, W. and C. Tait, 1821

Carson, Ciaran (trans.): *The Tain*, Penguin, 2008

Caygill, Marjorie: *Treasures of the British Museum*, BM, 1985

Chadwick, Nora K.: *The Age of the Saints in the Early Celtic Church*, Oxford, 1963

Colgrave, Bertram (ed.): *Two Lives of Saint Cuthbert*, Cambridge, 1985

Culling, Elizabeth: *What is Celtic Christianity?*, Grove, 1994

de Paor, Maire and Liam: *Early Christian Ireland*, Thames and Hudson, 1964

Fletcher, Richard: *The Conversion of Europe*, Fontana, 1997

Giles, J.A. (ed.): *The Works of Gildas and Nennius*, Bohn, 1841

Godfrey, C.J.: *The Church in Anglo-Saxon England*, Cambridge, 1962

Hamer, Richard (ed.): *A Choice of Anglo-Saxon Verse*, Faber, 1970

Heaney, Seamus: *Beowulf: A Verse Translation*, Norton, 2002

Hunter Blair, Peter: *An Introduction to Anglo-Saxon England*, Cambridge, 1959

Mayr-Harting, Henry: *The Coming of Christianity to Anglo-Saxon England*, Penn State UP, 2001

McCabe, Joseph: *Crises in the History of the Papacy*, Putnam's, 1916

Parbury, Kathleen: *The History of the Saints of Lindisfarne*, Frank Graham, 1970

Simeon of Durham (trans. Joseph Stevenson): *A History of the Church of Durham*, Llanerch, 1993

Stancliffe, Clare and Cambridge, Eric (eds.): *Oswald: Northumbrian King to European Saint*, Paul Watkins, 1995

Stenton, Frank: *Anglo-Saxon England*, Oxford, 1998

Tacitus: *On Britain and Germany*, Penguin, 1948

Webb, J.F. (ed.): *The Age of Bede*, Penguin, 1998

Young, Graeme: *Bamburgh Castle*, Bamburgh Research Project, 2003

Young, Simon: *A.D. 500: A Journey Through the Dark Isles of Britain and Ireland*, Phoenix, 2005

For more books from the Langley Press,
please visit our website at:

www.langleypress.co.uk.

Made in the USA
Columbia, SC
29 September 2024

43229277R00069